KGB CIA

Intelligence and Counter-Intelligence Operations

KGB
CIA

U.S. AIR FORCE

17976

976

CELINA BLEDOWSKA
and
JONATHAN BLOCH

Bison Books

PICTURES, PREVIOUS PAGE: Some areas of activity which have involved the KGB and CIA. A leader of the CIA-backed Contras (above); a Soviet 'trawler' with a suspicious array of aerials, trailing a Nato exercise in the North Atlantic (center left); an SR-71 spyplane flying over its base (center right); a miniature camera with special telephoto lens (bottom left); the Berlin Wall, symbol of a divided Europe (bottom right).

RIGHT: An actual set of KGB rendezvous instructions, given to the agent Douglas Britten by his Soviet controller.

Published by
Bison Books Ltd
176 Old Brompton Road
London SW5 OBA
England

Copyright © 1987 Bison Books Ltd

ISBN 0-86124-368-4

Printed in Hong Kong   Reprinted 1988

CONTENTS

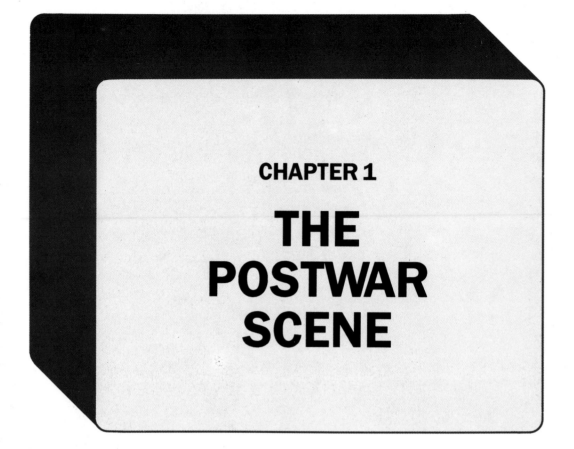

CHAPTER 1

THE POSTWAR SCENE

The 14 August 1945 marked the end of World War II, yet since that time a more secretive war has prevailed: the conflict between the security services of the two superpowers, the United States and the Soviet Union. The activities of spies have sometimes been presented as heroic and even romantic, but this secret war has been a brutal parade of ruthlessness, deceit and callous corruption.

The United States' Central Intelligence Agency (CIA) was set up as a direct result of American intelligence operations during World War II. In 1941, President Franklin D Roosevelt realized the need for a co-ordinator of intelligence to protect the interests of the United States, and he appointed William J Donovan (known in some circles as 'Wild Bill') to the position. Donovan was from the right background for the job. He had been decorated in World War I, was a millionaire, had served as assistant attorney general in the Justice Department and had also run as the Republican candidate for governor of

New York in 1932. He had travelled extensively before the war in Italy and Germany as well as in Britain and France. A British MI6 (Secret Intelligence Service) officer of the time said of him: 'We can do more through Donovan than any other individual . . . he can be trusted.' After Pearl Harbor Donovan's office changed its name and jurisdiction: he now became head of the Office of Strategic Services (OSS) and his headquarters moved to London. By the end of the war the OSS employed 13,000 people and had a budget of $37,000,000. There were four departments beneath Donovan – Support, Secretariat, Planning, and Overseas Missions. Each of these tiers spawned a further array of sections known as 'operation groups'. Many future directors and deputy directors of the CIA started their spying careers working for the OSS.

The OSS had grown largely out of the vital wartime need for overseas intelligence but Donovan was convinced of the need to re-

tain a similar type of organization for peace-time activities. In 1944 he wrote a memo to the President urging that 'the talent should not be dispersed'. Service chiefs and J Edgar Hoover (head of the Federal Bureau of Investigation – FBI) were not so keen to endorse a rival organization to their own intelligence services. In some quarters it was muttered that Donovan was trying to create a 'super spy organization' and 'an all-powerful intelligence service'. Unfortunately for Donovan Roosevelt died in April 1945. Donovan's style, the wildness noted in his nickname, had won him many powerful enemies including Harold Smith, the Budget director in President Truman's new administration. The OSS was disbanded and some of its numerous departments were reallocated within the State and War Departments. Other sections of the OSS simply ceased to exist. The retained units of the OSS drifted for some time. Their new parent organizations were unsure how to

ABOVE: President Franklin D Roosevelt, who set up the Office of Strategic Services (OSS) in 1941. After World War II, the OSS would evolve into the modern CIA.

LEFT: William J Donovan, millionaire head of the OSS throughout its four years' existence. Known as 'Wild Bill', Donovan made many enemies, and both he and his organization quickly fell from favor after Roosevelt's death in April 1945.

use them and there was little supervision or knowledge of quite what these ex-OSS groups were up to.

By September 1945 Navy Secretary James Forrestal realized that this state of affairs could not continue for much longer. He asked New York lawyer Ferdinand Eberstadt to submit a report which would define US requirements in the field of intelligence. Eberstadt complied and concluded that the United States needed a 'machine capable of waging war as well as peace'. As a result of this report President Truman set up the Central Intelligence Group (CIG), warning however that 'this country wanted no Gestapo under any guise . . . .' The Truman directive came into force in January 1946. As a check on the activities of the CIG, Truman constructed a four-man command group made up of the Secretaries of State, War, and the Navy, and Truman's personal representative. It was to this group, known as the National Intelligence Authority, that the CIG had to report. To celebrate the founding of the CIG Truman held a bizarre party, presenting his guests with black hats, cloaks and wooden daggers – it seems rather odd that an organization that was only supposed to collate information and not to spy should have been feted by the President in this way.

The CIG's first director, Admiral Sidney Souers, did not take the job too seriously

LEFT: Soviet tyrant Joseph Stalin (second from right) entertains diplomatic representatives of his British and American allies in 1945. Smiling 'Uncle Joe' did not share Western hopes for a democratic Europe after the war, and by 1947 the wartime allies were bitter enemies.

LEFT: Harry S Truman succeeded Roosevelt as US President in 1945. During the immediate postwar years he presided over the foundation of the current American intelligence set-up, including the CIA and the National Security Council (NSC).

either. He left after six months to become presidential assistant for intelligence affairs. His replacement, however, was of a different caliber. Lieutenant General Hoyt Vandenberg was a nephew of the influential Republican Senator Arthur Vandenberg and had ambitions to gain himself a fourth star and make something of the CIG in the process. Within a very short space of time Vandenberg was able to recruit 300 extra men. He also campaigned for the right to collect intelligence in Latin America, which had formerly been the task of the FBI. In August 1946 Vandenberg succeeded in gaining control from the War Department of the ex-OSS espionage and secret intelli-

gence organization, the Strategic Services Unit. This unit consisted of 1000 people, 600 of whom were attached to overseas field stations.

Other departments brought under the control of the CIG included the Office of Operations (OO), which was responsible for collecting information from American volunteers overseas, and the Foreign Broadcast Information Service (FBIS). The CIG also managed to liaise with the State Department and built close links with the fledgling code-breakers whose organization was later to become known as the National Security Agency (NSA). At this stage the CIG had a staff of 2000.

ABOVE: Lieutenant General Hoyt S Vandenberg, who took control of the Central Intelligence Group (CIG) in summer 1946 and soon turned it into a flourishing intelligence and espionage organization, the immediate forerunner of the CIA.

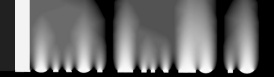

The war in Europe drew to an end on 7 May 1945 when Nazi Germany surrendered, overrun from the east by the Soviet Red Army and from the west by the United States and its Western allies. A temporary division of Europe into zones of occupation had been agreed between Soviet and Western leaders before the victory. As relations worsened in later years, the division became permanent, with an 'Iron Curtain' separating communist Eastern Europe, where Stalin installed pro-Soviet regimes, from the nations in the West allied to the United States.

In February 1945 the ailing President Roosevelt met Soviet leader Joseph Stalin at Yalta to discuss the future of Europe (left), but the reality of power lay with Soviet tanks (Berlin, April 1945, above) and guns (in Gdansk, Poland, below).

ABOVE: The ruined Reichstag building in the center of Berlin, May 1945. When the fighting stopped, Berlin was divided between the four occupying powers, Britain the United States, France and the Soviet Union. But it was deep inside the Soviet-controlled area of eastern Germany.

ABOVE AND RIGHT: Soviet and American troops fraternized cheerfully when they met on the Elbe at the end of April 1945, firm allies and joint conquerors of Nazi Germany. It was not destined to last.

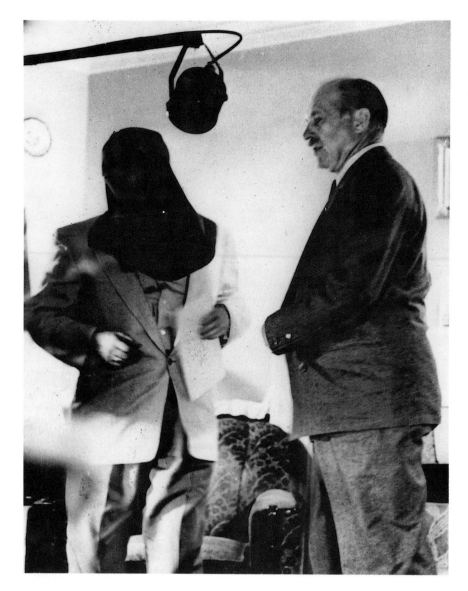

People's Commissariat of State Security (Narodnyi Kommissariat Gosudarstvennoi Bezonasnosti – NKGB). In 1946 all the Soviet commissariats were renamed 'ministries', so the NKVD became the Ministry of Internal Affairs (Ministerstvo Vnutrennikh Del – MVD) and the NKGB became the Ministry of State Security (Ministerstvo Gosudarstvennoi Bezonasnosti – MGB). Whereas in the United States the FBI was responsible for internal security and countering subversion, the CIA being restricted to external affairs, the MGB had control of both areas. Beria was, after Stalin, the most powerful man in the Soviet Union, running a vast empire of prison camps and using his secret police to crush any faint traces of dissent or opposition.

ABOVE: The man under the hood is Igor Gouzenko, the Soviet clerk whose defection in September 1945 revealed the existence of a widespread Soviet spy network in North America. Gouzenko is hooded to prevent his identification and possible elimination by Soviet agents as he starts a new life in Canada.

ABOVE RIGHT: Lavrenti Beria, head of the Soviet secret police under Stalin, with a prison camp empire under his control.

Meanwhile the rift between the United States and its former wartime ally the Soviet Union was growing. Relations were not helped by the revelation of extensive Soviet spying activities. In September 1945 Igor Gouzenko, a cypher clerk from the Soviet embassy in Ottawa, Canada, defected taking a collection of secret documents with him. Gouzenko's material revealed the existence of a major Soviet spy ring in Canada and the United States. In particular, high-ranking Canadian officials and scientists connected with the atom bomb project were implicated. A total of 22 people were arrested as Soviet agents. (Incidentally, Gouzenko pointed the finger at Anthony Blunt as a Soviet spy, but the British did nothing about him for 20 years.)

The position of the Soviet intelligence services was in many ways very different to that of the United States. At the end of the war, Stalin's henchman Lavrenti Beria ruled over a powerful network of secret police and agents centred on the People's Commissariat of Internal Affairs (Narodnyi Kommissariat Vnutrennikh Del – NKVD), and the

Within Beria's sphere came such secret projects as atomic weapons development. Not surprisingly, the race to match the United States' atomic capacity was a major priority of Soviet policy and it became the focus of espionage in the immediate postwar period. Like the United States, the Soviet Union benefitted from Nazi Germany's scientific and technological advances – both sides ransacked the V2 sites for materials and personnel. In 1946 the MVD was responsible for rounding up some 6000 scientists from the Soviet zone of Germany and taking them and their dependents to the Soviet Union where many of them stayed at least until 1951. But a more direct line to knowledge of the atom bomb lay in scientists or other personnel who

ABOVE: 2 Dzerzhinsky Square in the heart of Moscow, the central headquarters of the Soviet secret services and site of the notorious Lubyanka prison, in which so many opponents of the government have been held and tortured.

LEFT: Feliks Dzerzhinsky, for whom the square (above) was named. One of the original Bolshevik revolutionaries, Dzerzhinsky founded the first Soviet secret police force, the Cheka, at the time of the Revolution. He died in 1926, but his creation lived on, under ever changing names.

were prepared to pass on secrets to the Russians.

The Soviet intelligence service was very fortunate in the opportunities presented by the political conflicts of the 1930s and World War II. In the 1930s many educated people in the West identified with communism and the Soviet Union as the only force that could save the world from economic depression and fascism. It was easy for Soviet agents to recruit men who would subsequently rise to responsible positions and have access to secret material. Also, the alliance between the Soviet Union and the Western powers during the war confused allegiances, making it unclear whether communist sympathies should debar a person from a sensitive job, and whether passing information to the Soviets was an act of treachery at all.

As a result of this situation, there were 'atom spies' well positioned to keep the Soviets informed of every development in the West. Perhaps the most important was Klaus Fuchs, a German communist who had fled Hitler's reign of terror and whose ability as a nuclear physicist earned him a place on the Manhattan Project which developed the atom bomb. He later became head of the department of theoretical physics at the British atomic research establishment at Harwell. Fuchs passed secrets to the

ABOVE LEFT: A German V2 rocket ready for launch in 1945. Both America and the Soviet Union took scientists from the V2 project to advance their own military programs.

LEFT: Dr Klaus Fuchs, a brilliant scientist who passed atom-bomb secrets to the Soviet Union.

Soviets from 1941, and he was not arrested until 1950. Another prominent physicist was Alan Nunn May, who worked on the Anglo-Canadian atomic project and passed samples of the uranium used to Soviet agents. He was caught as a result of the Gouzenko revelations. Also passing on atom secrets were Julius and Ethel Rosenberg, eventually executed in the United States in 1953, and Donald Maclean, of whom more later (see Chapter 5). It is generally believed now that espionage in fact did little to speed up the Soviet nuclear

program – with such scientists as Andrei Sakharov they were quite capable of working it out for themselves. But the revelations about espionage certainly created panic and paranoia in the West.

1947 saw an escalation of intelligence activity on both sides of the world. The Soviet Union reorganized its services, creating a Committee of Information (KI) which was comprised of foreign intelligence units of the MVD and the army's intelligence organization. In the United States the National Security Act of 1947 gave birth to

ABOVE: A nuclear bomb explodes at Bikini atoll in one of America's first postwar tests. The Soviet Union was desperate to get its own bomb, and much of its espionage in the late 1940s was directed to that end.

ABOVE: Ethel and Julius Rosenberg, condemned to the electric chair as atom spies in 1953, despite worldwide protests. Americans blamed traitors for the Soviet development of the atom bomb and anti-communist hysteria gripped the United States.

RIGHT: Donald Maclean, one of the spies recruited by the Soviet Union at Cambridge University, England, in the 1930s. Maclean was posted to Britain's Washington embassy after the war and had access to American atom secrets, which he passed on to Moscow.

the CIA, reformed from the CIG. The act also established a governing body to replace the National Intelligence Authority. This new body was named the National Security Council (NSC). The President would be chairman of the NSC, giving a direct line of communication between the CIA and the White House. The new director of the CIA was Admiral Roscoe Hillenkoetter, who had worked for several years with navy intelligence and had set up a naval intelligence network in the Pacific. The National Security Act actually came into being on 18 September 1947. It gave the CIA intelligence collecting powers and made it answerable to the National Security Council. It also encompassed a wide range of "other functions" which the CIA could perform at the discretion of the NSC.

The duties of the CIA were defined as follows: to advise the NSC on intelligence activities of government departments and agencies relating to national security; to make recommendations to the NSC for the co-ordination of such intelligence activities;

to correlate and evaluate intelligence relating to national security; and to perform other such functions related to intelligence and affecting national security as the NSC may direct. In fact, the purely intelligence function was soon to become a secondary aspect of the CIA's activities.

Europe was to be the field in which the CIA first flexed its new muscles. Split between the West and the East, it seemed the great prize to be won or lost in the late 1940s. In Eastern Europe those countries which had been liberated from the Nazis by the Soviets were still playing host to their liberators. In some of these countries an active, if small, communist party had existed before the war, and during the war communist partisan groups had fought against the Nazis. Amid the destruction and chaos that reigned in the war's aftermath, it was to an extent natural that the local communists should emerge as a much strengthened force with a substantially increased measure of popular support. The MVD, however, systematically occupied

the interior ministries of the liberated countries and established its own secret police forces, loyal neither to the national government nor to the local communist party, but directly answerable to Moscow. By 1948 Beria's men were in a position to ensure puppet governments throughout Eastern Europe. A major casualty in Czechoslovakia was Foreign Minister Jan Masaryk. On 10 March 1948, Masaryk was found dead in the courtyard of his house. The official announcement claimed that he had committed suicide, yet it was widely believed that he had been murdered. Elections were held in Prague in May of that year, and initimidation ensured that communist candidates were elected unopposed. In Poland, meanwhile, communist leader Wladyslaw Gomulka proved too independent for Stalin's taste and was replaced. With the help of the MVD, Stalin was making sure of his empire.

LEFT: Admiral Roscoe Hillenkoetter, first director of the CIA in 1947.

BELOW: Czechoslovak Foreign Minister Jan Masaryk, who died in mysterious circumstances on 10 March 1948. It is widely believed that Masaryk was the victim of the Soviet secret police, intent on establishing Stalinist regimes throughout Eastern Europe and eliminating all potential opposition.

The main confrontation with the West came over Berlin, still divided between the wartime Allies but deep inside the Soviet zone of Germany. In June 1948 the Soviet Union blocked all entry to the city by land in an effort to force the other powers to quit, but the United States and to a lesser extent Britain kept the city supplied through an air corridor until the blockade was lifted.

Even before these disturbing events, the United States was worried about developments in Europe. The first meeting of the NSC was held in December 1947 and one of the main issues discussed was US foreign policy and the 'threat of communism'. There was particular concern about the strength of the Italian Communist Party. Many observers believed that the communists would win a majority in that country's first post-war elections, to be held in 1948. The matter was ably summed up by George Kennan, head of the State Department policy planning office at the time, who wrote: 'As far as Europe is concerned, Italy is the key point. If communists were to win elections there our whole position in the Mediterranean and possibly Europe as well would probably be undermined.'

So Italy became the first testing ground of the efficiency of the CIA. Hillenkoetter was ordered to set up a series of covert operations there to discredit the Communist Party and encourage other political groups. To carry out this instruction he established a

RIGHT: Berliners board an RAF aircraft bound for West Germany. Both the RAF and the USAF maintained an air link to West Berlin through all weathers to beat the Soviet blockade of the city in 1948.

Beating the Berlin blockade. Maintaining food supplies for half of a city (left) involved a massive operation by air. The Dakota proved an invaluable aircraft in carrying out this demanding task. Tempelhof Airport in Berlin (below) was the key center for the entire operation. The Soviet effort to force the Western Allies out of Berlin and incorporate the whole city in Soviet-occupied East Germany largely contributed to the worsening relationship between the United States and the Soviet Union, plunging the world into the era of the Cold War.

Special Procedures Group (SPG) under the Office of Special Operations (OSO), headed by James Jesus Angleton. An extremely bright but unapproachable man, Angleton became a dominant force in the Agency.

Before the mission began, Hillenkoetter asked the CIA's counsel whether the whole affair was legal and was told that it was not. But nevertheless it went ahead, giving the CIA its first opportunity to try out those talents for which it later became so famous. Posters and pamphlets were printed, anti-Soviet stories were planted in newpapers, and forged documents purportedly emanating from the Communist Party were also disclosed. It has been estimated that $75 million in covert financial aid was channelled to anti-communist parties and politicians. James Forrestal, Secretary of Defense, campaigned among wealthy Wall Street colleagues to raise the money. As well as this direct financial aid, letter campaigns were mounted, meetings and speeches were organized, and Truman threatened to withhold money from any Italian government which included com-

munists – a deadly threat to Italy's economic future.

In the event, the communists did not win the elections. Whether the CIA was responsible, or whether the Italians themselves, observing events in Eastern Europe, made up their own minds, is hard to say. The effort that the CIA had put into the mission was certainly massive by anyone's standards. Truman was delighted with the outcome and on 18 June 1948 the National Security Council issued directive NSC 10/2 which authorized the creation of a permanent organization for covert activities, to be called the Office of Policy Co-ordination (OPC). The CIA retained its own covert operations unit with the OSO. The directive instructed that 'activities had to be so carefully planned and carried out that any US Government responsibility for them is not evident to unauthorized persons and that if uncovered the US Government can plausibly disclaim any responsibility for them.' The first boss of this new group was Frank Wisner, an ex-OSS man.

In 1963 President Truman commented

BELOW: The Italian Communist Party was immensely popular in the aftermath of World War II, because of the part it had played in the resistance to Mussolini and the Germans. Its association with Moscow was a severe handicap for the party, however, particularly when the Soviet crackdown in Eastern Europe and the later revelations about Stalin's crimes blackened the image of the Soviet Union.

VOTA:
PER IL TUO PAESE

LEFT: An anti-communist Italian election poster calls on people to 'vote for their country.' The propaganda campaign mounted by the CIA in Italy in 1948 was one of the Agency's most successful efforts, persuading Italians not to vote for the Communist Party which many observers considered poised for victory in the democratic elections.

that: 'I never thought when I set up the CIA that it would be injected into peacetime cloak and dagger operations.' This comes from the man who held a cloak-and-dagger party at the CIA's inception! In 1949 the CIA Act was formally passed. The act exempted the CIA from all Federal laws that required the disclosure of 'functions, names, official titles, salaries or numbers of personnel employed by the agency'. The director was awarded staggering powers, including the right to 'spend money without regard to the provisions of law and regulations relating to the expenditure of government funds'. The act also allowed the director to bring in 100 aliens a year secretly.

This act and the setting up of the OPC basically set the stage for CIA covert actions for the next 40 years. The characters would change and some of the departments would merge, but essentially the 1949 act is still the charter which the CIA uses to allow itself the freedom to carry out covert operations.

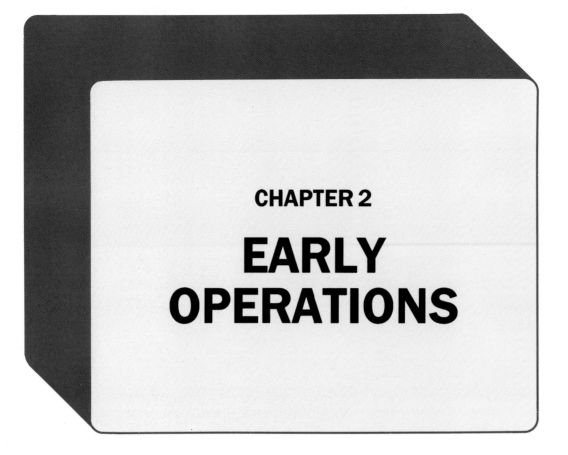

CHAPTER 2

EARLY OPERATIONS

During World War II, the OSS had devoted the greater part of its efforts to operations in enemy-occupied territory, particularly in liaison with local resistance groups. Not unnaturally, many ex-OSS operatives sought a similar role for themselves in the post-war confrontation with the Soviet Union. The result was a series of operations in Eastern Europe which could be termed active 'spy wars', as opposed to paper propaganda operations. The first of these, which could be taken as typical, was the Albanian fiasco.

Until 1948 Albania had been largely ignored as a little backward state, somewhere in the Balkans. The break between Yugoslavia's communist leader Josip Broz Tito and Stalin dramatically changed this state of affairs. In 1948 Stalin expelled Yugoslavia from Cominform, the organization of communist states. Tito and the Yugoslav partisans had successfully fought against the Nazis during World War II and Tito resented

Stalin's interference in the affairs of his country. Albania, as Yugoslavia's closest communist neighbor, had received aid from Tito. Yugoslavia trained Albania's professional workforce as well as supplying that country with essential materials and food. At one stage Tito described his relationship with Albania's leader Enver Hoxha as that of 'elder brother'. This was now all going to change, leaving Albania isolated and apparently vulnerable to the West.

At this time in the United States, the idea was growing that given the right sort of aid, anti-Soviet partisan groups, who were allegedly already working within the Eastern bloc countries, might be able to overthrow the post-war communist governments. Already during the spring of 1948 the US Chiefs of Staff had sent a colonel to the CIA in order to brief the Agency on the military's intelligence needs. Also former OSS veteran, Robert McDowell, in his capacity as advisor to the US Chiefs of Staff, had successfully convinced people that Stalin's grip on the Eastern bloc was somewhat shaky. McDowell also believed that if the Soviets clamped down too severely on the 'satellite states' resistance in those countries would grow. The Chiefs of Staff were fully behind McDowell's ideas and agreed with him that the United States must aid these 'partisan groups'. They also believed that US aid should be given to various emigré groups in order for them to launch any possible type of re-invasion of their respective countries. The CIA, as instructed by the Chiefs of Staff, participated in these schemes and obligingly dropped hundreds of agents behind the Iron Curtain. The CIA hoped that post-war Soviet chaos might occupy the minds of the MVD and thus allow the partisan groups to organize themselves into a full scale revolt against their governments.

McDowell has since been proven to have been hopelessly mistaken in his belief that a strong network of pro-American rebels existed in Eastern Europe. The emigré groups in the West wanted to believe that this was the case and therefore carried out a very good 'hard sell' on McDowell, but the reality was that Eastern Europe was too tired after five years of Nazi wartime occupation and further years of Soviet domination to be able to muster the strength required for such outrageous schemes.

As regards Albania, the pre-war ruler, King Zog, was in exile in Cairo, but it was claimed that many loyalists remained in Albania. Western Intelligence sources also knew that in some parts of Albania the

ABOVE: A Yugoslav partisan during the fight against the Nazi invaders in World War II. The struggle against the Germans developed an independent spirit in the Yugoslav communist supporters of Tito, and after the war they were not prepared to accept domination by Stalin.

LEFT: Royalist partisans in Yugoslavia during World War II, with their leader Mihailovic (center). The Royalists got short shrift from Tito's communists after the Germans had been driven out. The CIA sought to exploit the hostility of such groups against communist governments in Eastern Europe.

RIGHT: Queues outside a shop in Leipzig, East Germany. Throughout Soviet-occupied Eastern Europe, food shortages and general economic depression fuelled discontent in the post-war period.

BELOW: CIA equipment captured by the Czechs. These cameras and other instruments were attached to meteorological balloons and flown over Czechoslovakia to provide intelligence on military installations.

Britain's hostility to the communist government in Albania was partly due to an incident in October 1946 when two British destroyers struck mines in international waters close to Albania (top right, one of the ships, HMS *Volage*), and partly to Albanian support for communist guerrillas in the Greek Civil War (right).

communists under Enver Hoxha were having deep problems in trying to retain their power. Since 1947 the British Secret Intelligence Service (SIS, commonly known as MI6) had already been parachuting small groups of men into Albania to liaise with people on the ground. The Albanian loyalists, however, were not over impressed by small groups of Englishmen claiming that they had come to save them from Hoxha. The British had also been training small groups of guerrillas in refugee camps in Greece and Italy. Various small incur-

sions had been made into Albania, but in rather a desultory fashion.

The expulsion of Yugoslavia from Cominform in 1948 was the turning point in the Allies' perception of Albania. Hoxha started to expel his previous friends (the Yugoslav technicians and teachers) and the pro-Yugoslav Albanian foreign minister, Koci Xoxe, was arrested. The French minister Guy Menant, writing from Albania at this time, described conditions there as 'miserable' and added: 'War is the only thing they have to look forward to.' Suddenly the West began to look at Albania in a new light and realize the importance of its geographical position. Communist rebels were at that time being dispatched from Albania to a stricken Greece, which was in the middle of a bitter civil war. Italy was only 55 miles away and, as the elections in Italy had shown, that country was already a vulnerable point in the Western Alliance. And now, here was Albania, seemingly a Soviet stronghold, but also impoverished and vulnerable. The ideas planted in the minds of the CIA by the British MI6 gradually became more plausible and cohesive. Perhaps it might be possible with the help of King Zog and other emigrés to capture Albania for the West. By the end of 1948 British foreign minister Ernest Bevin had given the go-ahead for a small-scale military operation to destablize the Albanian communist government. A committee set up in Britain to fight the Cold War, called the Russia Committee, agreed on 16 December that there could be no question of taking action without the co-operation of the US Government, although the British were

ABOVE: King Zog of Albania reviews his troops in 1938. Ten years later, the King was living in exile in Cairo, but still dreaming of a return to the Albanian throne.

RIGHT: Yugoslav leader Josip Broz Tito, a great friend of the Albanian communist government until his split with Stalin in 1948. The Albanians stayed loyal to Moscow and broke off relations with Tito.

worried that 'the Americans were not always as forthcoming as we could have wished'. Accordingly William Hayter and Lord Jellicoe for the British Foreign Office flew to the United States to lobby support. There they met with OPC's Frank Wisner and Robert Joyce of the State Department.

The meeting agreed that neither government should come into the open about any possible action against the Albanian regime, but they could and would sponsor Albanian rebels. These rebels were to include wartime royalist and Balli Kombetar resistance leaders, most of whom were now based outside Albania: Midhat Frasheri was in Turkey, Abas Ermenji in Greece, Said Kryeziu and Abas Kupi in Italy. There was also a strong Albanian presence in Egypt, led by the exiled King Zog. The United States depended heavily on British experience and wartime knowledge of Albania.

In April 1949, Frank Wisner flew to London, to discuss locations for a possible training and lift-off base for the guerrillas. Initially a US base in Libya was chosen, but this was then turned down for a variety of reasons, and eventually the British-con-

trolled island of Malta was decided upon. Wisner, incidentally, had remarked to one of the MI6 men: 'Whenever we want to subvert any place we find that the British own an island within easy reach.' The MI6 man in question was a certain 'Kim' Philby.

The joint committee realized that an American was needed to liaise with the Albanians in order to demonstrate that this was to be a joint UK/US operation. The man that the OPC chose was a US Army reserve officer Robert Low. Low had wide experience of the Balkans and had also worked in Cairo during World War II. Even at this early stage of the plans there were signs that the operations might not prove as successful as was hoped. The Albanian refugees were made up of diverse factions, some of whom were still not talking to each other, even after several years of joint exile. Roughly speaking, the exiles were divided into three main camps, though other feuds, mainly of a family nature, also existed. For example, most tribes from northern Albania were Roman Catholic and, to a certain extent, better educated than their southern Moslem compatriots. There also existed the problem

of the fiercely anti-royalist Balli fighters. These were led by Abas Ermenji and had fought bravely during World War II. A further disjointed piece in this already complex jigsaw was the exiled King Zog himself. A compromise was reached in July 1949. Abas Kupi, the King's nominee, could be chairman of a military junta with Ermenji and another senior Albanian, Said Kryeziu, as deputies. An executive called the Albania National Committee was to be set up to promote the cause of a free Albania. The chairman of this executive was to be

ABOVE: Enver Hoxha (right) and his generals enter the Albanian capital Tirana in October 1944, ready to instal a communist regime. Hoxha was to be the only East European communist leader who remained a Stalinist even after destalinization in the Soviet Union itself.

the Balli leader Midhat Frasheri. It was only by much skilful diplomatic maneuvering that the King agreed to such a proposition. Zog then offered, as back-up, his entire Royal Guard without, one presumes, the one or two who were entrusted with the job of guarding Albania's pre-war gold reserve which was held in Zog's palace in Cairo.

On 14 July 1949 the first small band of guerrillas landed in Malta ready for training. Great secrecy surrounded these men once on Malta, though this at times was difficult to maintain, given the existing British military presence on the island. On 9 September the first team of Albanians left Malta for their homeland, on board a ship called the *Stormie Seas.* Italian coastguards monitored the little boat's progress and relayed information to the CIA. By October the group had reached Albania.

Tragically for the little team, on making contact with the local rebel groups, they were met by members of the Albanian police and security services. Messages were got out by a cousin of one of the Albanian liaison officers, and were received

at a British intelligence base on Corfu commanded by Alan Hare. Apparently three men had been killed, and others had been rounded up. James Angleton, who monitored this operation, believed that information had been leaked to the Soviets by some of the refugees living in the West. Already in 1917 when Felix Dzerzhinski had set up the Soviet secret service one of its first aims had been to penetrate every anti-communist group around. Angleton believed that there was no reason to suspect that the Soviets had changed their tactics. Some of the Albanian group finally got back to safety and were able to take part in further expeditions, but there was always some mishap and in some bizarre fashion the Albanian security forces always knew what was going to happen.

The OPC liaison officer working with the British was Michael Burke. Burke had worked in the OSS during the war and had been chosen by Frank Lindsay, the OPC European director, because of his impressive wartime record. Burke's first destination was Rome in order to supervise the selection of Albanians for the guerrilla activities. To this end he created a fictitious film company 'Imperial Films' which would give him a cover under which to work. At this stage Burke was not allowed to visit Malta. He was paid a salary of $15,000 per year, an astronomical figure in 1949.

Under the guidance of CIA advisor Lawrence de Neufville, the US High Commissioner in West Germany, John McCloy, came up with the idea of training the Albanian guerrillas there – they were to pose as a labor gang. The unit was called Company 4000 and consisted of 250 Albanian refugees commanded by Americans but with an underlying Albanian chain of command. One of Burke's tasks was to find a place for Company 4000 to train. Eventually a villa, known as the 'schloss' was found. It was situated outside Heidelberg, on the banks of the River Necker.

Despite these positive moves towards establishing a strong guerrilla force, CIA papers of the time reveal a hesitancy about the whole operation. On the one hand this hesitation is puzzling: the Soviet Union had successfully exploded its first atomic bomb in trials in September 1949 and therefore the influence of the Cold War warriors surrounding both the White House and 10 Downing Street would provide an even greater impetus for the Albanian operation to succeed. On the other hand, a CIA document of December 1949 reveals that the different departments within the US Administration, including the CIA, had all reached different conclusions as to the fate of Hoxha and therefore had in fact made no definite assertions as to the fate of Albania. Also the evident strength of Stalin had made some people act slightly more cautiously than the 'action boys' in the OPC would believe. None of these doubts was transmitted to the unfortunate Albanian guerrillas, however, at that moment being trained by the Allies.

Despite the unease in December 1949, the NSC reported to President Truman that: 'The United States should do what it can practicably, particularly through covert operations and propaganda, to keep alive the anti-communist sentiment and hope of those making up the non-communist majorities in the satellite countries. To do less would be to sacrifice the moral basis of the US leadership of free people.'

1950 saw the mood of the American people change dramatically. They were angry that the Soviet Union appeared to be getting the upper hand in world domination and felt that their own government had not been trying hard enough. This mood was

helped along by Senator Joe McCarthy, who accused 81 members of the State Department of having acted disloyally and also referred frequently to 'communists within the US Government'. Dean Acheson was attacked for being friends with the spy Alger Hiss and a Senate sub-committee started hearings on State Department officials. The hunt was up, with the hounds baying for blood – the hounds at that time being a vast proportion of the American people led by an unpleasant master in the shape of Joe McCarthy. The prevailing

ABOVE: James Angleton, one of the most celebrated figures in the history of the CIA. He was especially renowned for his counter-espionage work, keeping the CIA almost completely free of double agents. Angleton died in 1987.

The sudden exposure of the atom spies and the revelation of Soviet agents working in government departments spurred Senator Joseph McCarthy to embark upon a well-publicised witch-hunt of communists in high places. Working mainly through his chairmanship of the Senate Investigations Committee, he charged that communists and 'fellow travellers' had comprehensively infiltrated US governmental agencies. Where he failed to secure an outright conviction or public confession he ensured that his (often innocent) victims were broken by the attendant publicity surrounding the investigations. McCarthy himself was formally censured by the Senate in 1954 for his excessive behaviour and died three years later a discredited man.

RIGHT: Wisconsin Senator Joe McCarthy, leader of the anti-communist witchhunt of the early 1950s.
BELOW: McCarthy enjoyed the fervid support of conservative Americans

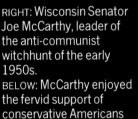

LEFT: The McCarthy hearings in progress. Convinced that communist subversion threatened the American way of life, the senator used every trick to smear those he suspected. Producing a photo (below) showing a member of the administration standing alongside a communist was enough for McCarthy to denounce the man himself as a subversive.

ABOVE: As a former friend of the spy Alger Hiss and a leading figure in the State Department, it was almost inevitable that Dean Acheson should be a target for the anti-communist hysteria sweeping through America in the 1950s.

RIGHT: A market day in a Moslem area of Albania. Western hopes that the peasants would rise up against their communist masters proved ill-founded.

between the Greeks and the British. The expedition had hoped to go overland from Greece into Albania but no one had explained to the Greek intelligence services why these Albanians had suddenly appeared in their country. Given that Greece was strongly suspicious of Albanians thanks to Hoxha's training of communist partisans during the Greek Civil War, the Greek police, not surprisingly, panicked and arrested the party. After much difficulty the men were released and delivered to a 'safe house' but the harm had been done, and the team had to lie low for some time. A further attempt was then made at an overland penetration of Albania. This time the men successfully entered Albania. Unfortunately though, as in previous expeditions, few of the original party returned. Those that did came back far earlier than expected. The stories the men brought back were sobering: it was hard to move around Albania in small groups and all the time they felt as if the Albanian secret police was briefed on their every move.

The Albanians still training in Malta started to have grave doubts as to the feasibility of their mission. At this stage certain of those who were in charge of training the Albanians began to have doubts too. Was the operation being put forward, despite the gloomy tales from Albania, merely to please the MI6 bosses in Broadway and the CIA/OPC chiefs in the Lincoln Building, Washington? If so, was this not some ghastly experiment using live humans as bait? Another suspicion which crossed their minds was that this was a battle for supremacy between MI6 on the one hand and the OPC on the other. By 1950 the British secret services were feeling the effects of Britain's economic decline. The same did not apply to the OPC. Their abundance of money has been described in some quarters as 'obscene'. Also, in terms of scientific development for secret operations the United States was streets ahead. The British had to succeed in this operation or be doomed to remain the junior partner of the United States for ever.

In 1950 Wisner appointed Gratian Yasevich as commander of the Albanian mission. Yasevich could speak Serbo-Croat and knew the Balkan area well. He also worked closely with Kim Philby co-ordinating the US and British operations. By June 1950 South Korea had been invaded by forces from the North. US intelligence saw this action as a legitimation of their Albanian guerrilla activities and tried to speed up the operation. The problem still existed of how to get men into Albania. Eventually it was

mood decided the CIA, and the OPC were ordered to get the Albanian operation up and running.

The 'schloss' training regime was now started in earnest. Men were recruited from Displaced Persons (DP) camps and pulled into shape. But even in these surroundings pro- and anti-royalist sentiments and politics kept on appearing.

Meanwhile the men training under the British in Malta were about to start their second foray into Albania. The survivors of the first expedition had now rejoined them after having been released from Greek jails where they had been held as a result of their illegal entry into Greece from Albania. The second expedition failed farcically. This time the reason was lack of negotiation

decided to fly them in; using small un-marked craft the OPC were reasonably con-fident that the flights could be made unobtrusive. Also, more importantly in terms of international relations, American credi-bility as observers of international law in peacetime would not be damaged. MI6 man Harold Perkins hit upon the idea of using Polish pilots for the mission. England at this stage still had many Polish pilots living on her soil, many of whom had fought in the Battle of Britain and had proved themselves to be outstandingly courageous. Chillingly, the pilots were given cyanide pills in case of capture.

Extensive training was also taking place in the Heidelberg 'schloss'. Extra US in-structors had been brought over, but when Albanian leaders Kupi and Ermenji visited the school they were worried that the men had not received long enough training. A month later 16 men left Germany en route for Greece. Unfortunately, yet again some-one had bungled the Greek liaison, so rather than risk 16 mysterious Albanians hanging around a Greek airport, the unfortunate men had to be sent back to Germany. It was hardly an auspicious omen for any heroic liberation struggle. The scheme was re-started, this time with nine rather than 16

BELOW: A street scene in Albania, graphically illustrating the economic backwardness and shabbiness of life under Enver Hoxha.

men. The pilots had terrible difficulty in finding the right drop-off spot in Albania, but eventually the infiltrators decided to jump anyway and risk it. Yet again a trap had been set and all but two of the men were captured by waiting security forces. In retaliation for the escape of one of the men, Adem Gjura, the security police murdered his whole family, including cousins. Gjura and his colleague reached Yugoslavia safely where he was imprisoned for 17 years. While in Yugoslavia he tried to send out a message to warn the mission's commanders about the 'reception committee', but he was never sure if the message had been received.

Despite these horrific setbacks the OPC continued with its operations. Further recruits were trained in the 'schloss'. More money was pumped into the operation and channelled through Rome. In June 1951 another drop was made of 16 men. Yet again the tragic fate of their comrades befell them. Those who were not shot on the spot were put on parade in Tirana for a show trial. It is believed that all those who were not sentenced to death met their end at the hands of the Albanian secret police. After the October 1951 trial morale in the Albanian camp was extremely low. Arguments broke out again between the royalist and republican sides. The British attempted to train further groups of Albanians in Britain itself, on the rugged terrain of Dartmoor. The training failed; the men were just not fit enough. The Dartmoor session was the last straw for the British: they pulled out of the Albanian nightmare.

Not so the CIA. They had their hopes pinned on one guerrilla in particular – Hamit Matjani – who had so far survived every obstacle which had come his way. During 1952 men were trained with Matjani as their leader. The men were transferred from Germany to the Greek island of Kalanissia, now a secret CIA base. King Zog released more men from his personal Royal Guard to join the mission. Even at this stage the CIA still

BELOW: Harold 'Kim' Philby, perhaps the supreme double agent. His high mental abilities, plus his perfectly 'appropriate' social background, earned him a rapid rise through the British intelligence service, but he was in fact a totally dedicated communist, tireless in his work for the Soviet cause.

believed that there was some realistic chance of Hoxha's regime being toppled. Throughout 1952 small groups of men successfully landed in Albania and managed to build up small networks of contact. Stalin died on 5 March 1953, and this for the CIA was seen as a good omen. But on New Year's Eve 1953 Albanian radio revealed that all the men flown into Albania had been captured and that for almost two years the secret police had been duping the CIA. Matjani had been held prisoner almost from the time he had landed in Albania. The others had been or were to be shot. Hundreds of their relatives were also killed.

The reasons why the whole operation went so disastrously wrong are numerous, but most intelligence experts agree that the main reason was Harold 'Kim' Philby. Philby has now been exposed as a traitor and currently lives in Moscow, but in 1949 few people doubted his mettle. He was the perfect gentleman. Cambridge educated, son of a maverick but famous father, with many friends inside the 'Service', bright, witty and amusing – in fact the perfect caricature of the MI6 man. It was this 'perfect gentleman' who in 1949 became the British intelligence representative in the United States. He linked with James Angleton and also with the OPC. Philby was also the joint commander of the Albanian operation, and frequently sat in on meetings at the MI6 offices in the British embassy in Washington. Robert Low was suspicious of a leak but did not know where to point the finger. He said: 'It was obvious there was a leak somewhere. The communists knew too much.' Philby was recalled to London in 1951, after the defection of Burgess and MacLean to the Soviet Union. Walter Bedell Smith, CIA boss from October 1950, had started to become suspicious of Philby and threatened to break off the American-British intelligence relationship unless he was removed. Once back in London, Philby was interrogated, but successfully managed to blind his questioners. Of his time in Washington Philby himself says: 'The more visitors I had in Washington, the more pies I got my finger into. That after all was my aim in life.' Philby has never actually confessed to the Albanian massacre but by piecing together his position, his contacts, the Washington era and the later revelations that he was a traitor, plus the fact that the Albanian secret police were so well briefed as to the landing spots of the emigré guerrillas, one can suppose that Philby was largely responsible for the murder of over 300 men, women and children.

The other reasons for the fiasco include

ABOVE: General Walter Bedell Smith, director of the CIA from 1950 to 1953. Smith was highly suspicious of Philby and insisted on his removal from Washington as a condition of continuing intelligence co-operation between the United States and Britain.

the unreal bullishness of both the CIA and MI6. Why did they take so long to read the signals that the expeditions were doomed to failure? Were they so caught up in their own Cold War propaganda that they could no longer clearly evaluate a situation? The OPC European director at that time, Frank Lindsay, today says: 'It was unethical as well as foolish to carry on sacrificing human lives in the operation's later stages.'

Of course the main victims of this unhappy espisode were the Albanians themselves. Egged on by both intelligence services these men set forth on a mission which otherwise they would never have attempted. Philby was the traitor but neither MI6 nor the CIA was totally innocent.

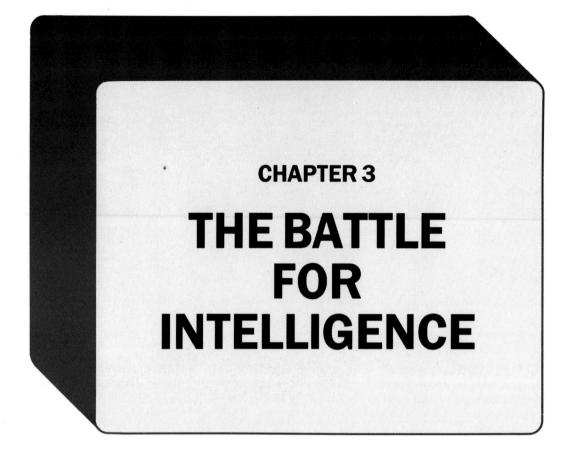

CHAPTER 3

THE BATTLE FOR INTELLIGENCE

If an intelligence agency is to be seen as working efficiently it has to be seen to be working. In order to be seen to be working it must first of all convince its own government and only secondly convince the enemy. This moral appears to be the guiding light for both the US and Soviet intelligence agencies from the 1950s up until the present day. To carry out these functions the agency must be properly organized.

In 1950 Admiral Hillenkoetter was replaced as director of the CIA by General Walter Bedell Smith. It was Smith who reshaped the Agency along the lines which it follows today. Smith established three Directorates in order to rid the Agency of some of the muddle and crossover work which it had been involved in to 1950. By 1952 the Office of Policy Co-ordination and the Office of Special Operations had been united into one department – the Directorate of Plans. Allen Dulles was placed in

charge of this Directorate. Frank Wisner became deputy director of plans with Richard Helms as chief of operations. A Directorate of Intelligence was established in order to promote the CIA's public face. An Office of National Estimates (ONE) came under this jurisdiction in order to provide analysis and estimates within the Agency. Other analytical offices included the Office of Scientific Intelligence (OSI) and the Office for Current Intelligence (OCI). Finance and logistics were provided by the Directorate of Support (DDS) later known as the Directorate of Administration (DDA).

By the end of 1952 the CIA employed 10,000 people and seemed to have limitless finance. In 1953 Eisenhower became President of the United States and appointed General Smith to his staff. Allen Dulles was promoted to director of the CIA, just coinciding with his brother John Foster Dulles becoming Secretary of State. Allen Dulles's career in intelligence dated back as

LEFT: President Dwight D Eisenhower (left) and his Secretary of State John Foster Dulles (center) entertain a diplomatic guest. Eisenhower and Dulles were committed to the world struggle against communism and expected the CIA to play an active role.

BELOW: Allen Dulles, director of the CIA during the 1950s. Brother of Eisenhower's Secretary of State, Allen Dulles was considered to be one of the most successful of the CIA's chiefs.

far as World War I. In World War II he had served with the OSS. He was fascinated by operational case details, to the extent that he was nicknamed 'the great white case elephant'. It was under Dulles that what is often described as the Agency's 'halycon' period started.

Dulles saw his mission as to 'roll back communism'. The attempt at active operations in Eastern Europe was replaced by a massive propaganda effort aimed in the same direction. Radio Liberty was founded, as well as the German-based Radio Free Europe (RFE). Radio Free Europe cost the Agency $30 million a year and was mainly staffed by East European emigrés and intellectuals. Religious broadcasts were transmitted on RFE into Eastern Europe, as well as other diverse programs. The total budget for the Directorate of Plans amounted to a staggering $82 million.

The CIA's long-term plans involved the building of several 'institutes' to promote 'the word according to the CIA'. They spent $1 million on funding and establishing the Congress for Cultural Freedom. The Center for International Studies in Massachusetts Institute of Technology was established with a $300,000 grant from the Agency. The Center was to run for a total of 16 years. Also at this time the CIA chief of internal organization gave Walter Reuther, of the United Auto Workers, $50,000 in covert funds. This money eventually found its way to non-Communist labor unions in West Germany.

Of course, the Soviet Union aided and promoted large labor unions in Western Europe, especially those in France and Italy

which were already dominated by the communist parties. But among the world labor organizations, the CIA was not reticent. In the 1970s it was revealed that the CIA had been behind the vast International Confederation of Free Trade Unions (ICFTU). As well as trying to control labor operations in Europe, ICFTU launched regional operations throughout the Third World. The man behind a lot of these schemes was Arthur Goldberg, who had been head of OSS labor operations and then went on to be Secretary of Labor and a Supreme Court Justice.

Essentially, the purpose of these 'front' organizations was to transmit propaganda without looking like propaganda organizations. On the one hand they had to appear in the role of liberal friends to all people and on the other hand they could be used to disseminate information which, had it emanated from the direct source, would have immediately been discredited. As well

as labor organizations, the CIA channelled funds to youth movements. The European Youth Campaign, for example, received £1,300,000 from the CIA between 1951 and 1959. This was confirmed in 1975 by Tom Braden, an ex-CIA officer who had served in the CIA's International Organizations division.

While the CIA reorganized and mounted its propaganda offensive, its counterpart in the Soviet Union had been undergoing major reconstruction. In the last years of Stalin's rule, in the early 1950s, the dictator had become even more paranoid than before and Beria's secret police had been ever more inventive in its 'discovery' of plots and thorough in its reign of terror. But Beria himself was far from secure. According to Soviet leader Nikita Khrushchev's later account, Stalin ordered Semen Ignatiev, director of the MGB, to fabricate evidence against a number of Moscow physicians, most of them Jewish, who were accused of

trying to murder the Soviet leader. Ignatiev was reportedly told by Stalin that 'if you don't obtain confessions from the doctors, we will shorten you by a head'. It was claimed that Stalin was intending to remove Beria from power by accusing him of incompetence in not discovering the 'plot'. But Stalin died on 5 March 1953, before this last purge could be carried out. On his death the US ambassador to the Soviet Union, George Kennan, commented: 'If he (Stalin) was not a madman before he died, he was just this side of madness.' There have been some suspicions that Beria himself, realiz-

ABOVE AND ABOVE LEFT: Europe was not the only continent where the CIA used radio to broadcast its message. Voice of America offered the same service to Asia, hoping to reach even the illiterate peasant populations.

LEFT: American labor leader Arthur Goldberg and wife on a visit to Israel. Goldberg was responsible for organizing worldwide anti-communist labor unions with money provided by the CIA.

RIGHT: Stalin lies in state after his death in March 1953, watched by his erstwhile colleagues, including police chief Beria (second from right) and future premier Khrushchev (second from left). A bitter power struggle followed between Beria and communist party leaders; Beria lost and was soon executed.

ABOVE: Georgi Malenkov, Stalin's immediate successor, addresses the Supreme Soviet. Beria sits uncomfortably alongside Khrushchev at the back of the podium.

ing that he was under threat, had a direct hand in Stalin's death.

It seemed likely that Beria would win the ensuing power struggle to rule the Soviet Union, for his control of the secret police apparently gave him the trump card. But the other members of the Politburo, with Khrushchev playing an important role, out-maneuvered Beria and in June 1953 he was arrested. On 24 December *Pravda* announced that he had been executed. The party leadership then took its revenge on the MGB which had for so long terrorized

them as much as it had the ordinary Soviet citizen. Formally, the organization was downgraded from a ministry to a state committee, becoming the Committee for State Security (Komitet Gosudarstennoi Bezopasnasti – KGB). Its powers were considerably reduced – it could no longer arrest party members or conduct its own trials, and most of the labor camps were taken out of its control. The number of employees of the KGB was also much smaller than its predecessor. The MVD, for its part, became the ministry in control of the ordinary police.

BELOW: By the time this picture was taken in 1957, Khrushchev (center) had denounced Stalin's crimes and cut down the power of the secret service, now known as the KGB. In particular, he denied the secret police power over communist party members.

ABOVE: A U2 spyplane cruising at high altitude. It was thought that flying at 85,000 feet would make the aircraft immune to Soviet air defenses, but surface-to-air missile technology eventually caught up and overtook the spyplane.

The head of the new KGB was General Ivan Serov, previously security chief in Khrushchev's Ukraine, but overall control of state security lay with the more powerful figure of Aleksander Shelepin. In 1958, Shelepin was to take over direct control of the KGB himself.

Despite these internal preoccupations, the Soviets were by no means idle in the fields of propaganda and intelligence work during these years. From 1948 until 1953 MGB agents posing as Soviet newsmen mounted an intense disinformation campaign against the United States and US involvement in Japan, for example. They had also found time to plant 130 listening devices in US embassies, and in 1952 a further 44 devices were placed in the US embassy in Moscow.

The Soviets had no match for the propaganda coup achieved by the CIA in 1956, however, when it obtained a copy of Khrushchev's 'secret' speech delivered to a closed session of the 20th Party Congress, in which the Soviet leader denounced Stalin's crimes and his methods of ruling the country. The KGB knew that if the speech was released to the West, it would play into the hands of the CIA who would seize upon it as a justification of all their covert actions. Also, how could the KGB ensure that the West did not doctor and exaggerate the disgraceful list of crimes which Khrushchev attributed to Stalin?

In fact, via James Angleton a copy of the speech did fall into the hands of the CIA. How it reached Angleton is another question. One school of thought is convinced that the West German intelligence organization run by Reinhard Gehlen obtained the copy and passed it on. Others claim that Angleton obtained the speech from close contacts with the Israeli secret service, Mossad. Mossad, in turn, is suspected of having obtained the speech through contacts in Poland.

Once it had got a copy of the speech, the CIA could not make up its mind what to do with it. Soviet-watcher Dr Ray Cline, though convinced of the document's accuracy, did not want it to be released in sections, preferring that the document should be released in full. Angleton and Wisner on the other hand thought that maximum propaganda effect could be gained by releasing the speech in sections. A huge argument raged for days at the Directorate of Plans' Headquarters, the 'Reflecting Pool,' in Washington. Eventually the speech was released in full and published in the *New York Times*. To the present day there have been many debates as to the legitimacy of the copy of the speech released and as to whether the CIA had actually doctored it. Naturally enough, the Agency denies any such implications.

Also in 1956, the CIA began a quite new kind of spy project that looked toward the

LEFT: Eisenhower as Allied commander in World War II. His background as a military leader did not necessarily prepare Eisenhower well for the subtleties of world diplomacy, and in the U2 affair he was undoubtedly outwitted by the wily Khrushchev, who drew the maximum political advantage from the hand fate had dealt him.

future and opened up fresh fields of espionage. The Agency had always lacked a secure and dependable way in which to spy directly on the Soviet Union. Reliance on agents was dangerous and the information they could collect was limited. Eisenhower had already publicly floated the idea that one way to set disarmament in motion would be to allow monitored viewing by each side of the other's military establishments, and suggested that aerial photography might be the means of carrying this out. Khrushchev described the proposal as 'pure fantasy'. But aerial surveillance was

the line of development that the CIA chose to pursue, producing the U2 reconnaissance aircraft.

The aim of the U2 project was to fly over the Soviet Union and photograph missile and defense-related installations. In cooperation with the air force the CIA recruited pilots, one of whom was Gary Powers. Altogether about 100 pilots were chosen. The CIA used among other places the Incirlik Air Base near Adana in Turkey as a base from which to make the reconnaissance flights, and for this work Powers and his colleagues were paid $30,000. Powers

SPY PLANES

In 1952 the United States began to consider the use of high-altitude reconnaissance aircraft to solve the problem of obtaining intelligence from behind the iron Curtain. The US project, developed with $54 million of CIA funding, aimed at producing an aircraft to overfly the Soviet Union. The first such flight took place in July 1956, and 30 more missions were completed before Gary Powers was shot down by an SA-2 missile on 1 May 1960. Despite this debacle U2s were used to great effect during the Cuban missile crisis in 1962; they provided the Americans with

irrefutable photographic evidence of the existence of Soviet ballistic missile sites on Cuba. The U2 continued in service until 1976, but in 1964 the prototype of the more advanced SR-71 Blackbird (CIA designation A-12) made its first flight. With a cruising speed of Mach 3, the SR-71 has remained an important intelligence tool despite the increasing use of spy satellites.

TOP AND TOP RIGHT: The Lockheed SR-71 Blackbird.
ABOVE: An earlier spyplane, the RB-57.
RIGHT: The notorious U2 reconnaissance plane in flight.

himself made the first flight over the Soviet Union in November 1956. For four years the U2 spy flights continued, bringing back information and photographs of 'airfields, aircraft, missiles, missile testing and training, special weapons storage, submarine production, atomic production and aircraft deployments.' The U2 was an extremely flimsily built aircraft, but despite its fragility the plane could cruise at the astonishingly high altitude of 85,000 feet, thus avoiding any problems with turbulent weather.

What was to prove a fatal U2 flight over

the Soviet Union took place on 1 May 1960 and once more Powers was the pilot. As he flew over Sverdlovsk, Powers was brought down by a Soviet SA-2 missile. Even worse for the CIA, he was neither killed in the crash nor took the cyanide pill with which he had been issued. With Powers a prisoner in their hands, the Soviets were in a position to carry out a magnificent diplomatic coup. An international summit was scheduled to take place on 16 May, with Eisenhower, Khrushchev and the French and British leaders participating, so it was a focal moment in superpower relations. To gain maximum advantage from the situation, Khrushchev first allowed Eisenhower to deny publicly that spy flights were being authorized. The Soviet leader then produced Powers at a press conference on 7 May and the American President was revealed as a liar. The summit conference was abandoned in an atmosphere of mutual antagonism and distrust.

One of the major questions about this incident, which has never been satisfactorily resolved, is the issue of who authorized a spy flight at that particularly sensitive juncture in East-West relations – it was only the thirtieth flight in four years. The Senate Foreign Relations Committee returned a verdict that: 'Neither the President, the Secretary of State, nor the Secretary of De-

The Soviet Union gave the most publicity possible to their shooting down of the U2 spyplane. An exhibition on the U2 was mounted in Moscow's Gorki Park (right), attracting large crowds.
The aircraft's camera (on exhibition, above) was designed to take pictures through seven different windows in the fuselage, and could carry enough film to photograph a strip of territory 2200 miles long.

fense knew that the particular flight was in the air.' The finger then points to the CIA camp. Allen Dulles refused to testify to the Foreign Relations Committee, either on or off the record. Informed Washington opinion at the time believed that Dulles had arranged for a sympathetic individual to be located at the White House, possibly someone from the NSC Special Group. Dulles could then claim that he had received authorization from the White House, but the authorization need not have come from that President himself. Possibly Dulles had been trying to steamroller the Soviets at the forthcoming conference, because obviously their radars would have picked up the U2, yet none of this would have been public knowledge – a classic example of the two agencies playing games with each other. Unfortunately for Dulles the mission had failed in a very public way.

As for Powers, he was imprisoned for 18 months, though he had been sentenced to 10 years. The reason for his early release was the capture of the wily Rudolf Abel, which in turn led to the first 'spy-swap'. Rudolf Abel was a somewhat bizarre character, with his sinister elongated features. He is alleged to have been born as

ABOVE: President Eisenhower addresses Congress, with Vice-President Richard M Nixon seated behind him. Nixon's chances of election to the presidency in 1960 were severely compromised by the U2 fiasco.

LEFT: The unfortunate Francis Gary Powers, pilot of the U2 shot down on 1 May 1960. He was criticized in some quarters for his failure to commit suicide after his plane crashed, allowing the Soviets to take him prisoner. This photo was taken by his captors.

William Fisher in England in 1903. His father had been a friend of Lenin and eventually moved to the Soviet Union. Rudolf joined the Soviet Communist Party in 1920 and, as a gifted linguist, was soon recruited for intelligence work. He obviously displayed a flair for it, since he was sent to Berlin to the Technische Hochschule to study. He returned to Moscow after graduating and continued his training in military espionage. In 1949, after taking on the alias of Andrew Kayotis, a US citizen who had died while visiting relatives in Lithuania, Abel entered Quebec, Canada. Once safely in Canada Abel adopted a new persona, calling himself Emil R Goldfus; he also found himself a new profession, that of photographer. Armed with his new identity Abel crossed the Canada/US border, and set himself up with

a small business in Brooklyn. From there he successfully conducted espionage activities for a number of years. In 1957, however, he was finally arrested in a New York hotel room where he was staying under yet another alias, 'Martin Collins'. Abel refused to be 'turned' and gave nothing away; he was sentenced to 30 years' imprisonment.

But Abel was lucky in that fate intervened on his behalf. James Donovan, a New York attorney and a former OSS man, was instructed in 1962 to see if it were possible to arrange a 'swap' for Powers. Donovan agreed to the deal and set up negotiations with the Soviet Union. The contacts between the two sides took place through the medium of letters. Donovan started to receive correspondence from someone claiming to be Helen Abel, supposedly the wife of the Soviet spy. He passed the letters on to CIA general counsel Lawrence Houston who prepared a response. Eventually Donovan went to Berlin to set up the final parts of the deal. Technically he travelled as a private US citizen with no special government protection. In February 1962 Gary Powers was exchanged for Rudolf Abel at the East German checkpoint of Glienicker Bridge. This was to be the first of many such swaps on the bridge with little change to the routine, except that the size of the security forces overseeing each successive swap has increased. Rudolph Abel died in the Soviet Union in 1971.

The 1950s, then, in terms of propaganda and espionage, was a period of expansion and also the laying of foundations for future operations. With the establishment of the various CIA-backed foundations and the Soviet investment in Western trade unions both sides had succeeded in building strong and lasting powerbases. One of the main differences in operations during this period was that the Soviet leaders knew what the KGB was involved in, whereas the CIA had not necessarily informed the US Administration of what exactly was going on. The KGB has often been shown to have been more brutal in its methods, but at the CIA training camp at Camp Peary, Virginia, in the mid-1950s an instructor once told his class: 'On occasions it has been necessary to physically eliminate someone who was a threat to the Agency.' Other officers within the CIA disagree with this point of view.

During the time when these tools of propaganda were being put in place, major events occurred elsewhere which changed the world completely and have played a major part in policy and decision-making today. These include the CIA interventions in Iran, Guatemala and Cuba.

BELOW: Soviet spy Rudolf Abel in handcuffs after his arrest by the FBI in 1957. Abel resisted interrogation very well and many details of his activities remain obscure. He was returned to the Soviet Union in exchange for U2 pilot Gary Powers in February 1962, the first ever 'spy swap.'

ABOVE: A tense moment during a spy swap at the Glienicker Bridge checkpoint, Berlin. It was here that Powers and Abel were exchanged in 1962.

LEFT: Gary Powers poses for the cameras with a model of a U2 after his return from the Soviet Union. Powers was a pilot, not a spy, and in swapping him for Abel, a senior Soviet agent, the United States definitely lost out on the deal.

CHAPTER 4

CIA INTERVENTION

In the 1950s evidence first emerged of CIA intervention in the internal affairs of countries outside the Soviet block to unseat established governments and replace them by anti-communist rulers favorable to American interests. In 1953, the target was Iran.

For two years, since 1951, effective power in Iran had rested with Prime Minister Mohammed Mossadegh, who had reduced the young Shah, Mohammed Reza Pahlavi, to a virtual figurehead. Mossadegh rode a wave of popular nationalist enthusiasm, supported, but in no sense dominated, by the local communist party, the Tudeh. His most popular move was his initial decision to nationalize the powerful British-owned Anglo-Iranian Oil Company which many Iranians believed was milking the nation's wealth and offering little in return. The British were outraged by this measure, just as they would be later when Nasser nationalized the Suez Canal in 1956, but

they were incapable of getting rid of Mossadegh themselves. With American support, they mounted an economic blockade which had a critical effect on the Iranian economy, but Prime Minister Winston Churchill wanted more direct action. In 1952 the British first put out feelers to see if an operation could be mounted by the CIA. The Truman Administration was cautious about such an adventure, however, and nothing happened until the following year, when John Foster Dulles was installed as Secretary of State. To Dulles, Iran appeared a clear case of Soviet-orchestrated communist subversion. He was also not unaware that this was an opportunity to move into an area that had previously been a British preserve. So the CIA was instructed to carry out the task of ousting Mossadegh.

The man put in charge of the operation was Kermit ('Kim') Roosevelt, grandson of President Theodore Roosevelt (1858-1919). Kim had left Harvard to work in the OSS

ABOVE: Iranian Prime Minister Mohammed Mossadegh whose action in nationalizing British petroleum interests precipitated a crisis. Mossadegh was not a communist but he did enjoy the support of the Tudeh, Iran's communist movement.

LEFT: President Truman and Prime Minister Winston Churchill engage in a friendly chat. Churchill was not successful, however, in his efforts to persuade Truman that action should be taken against Mossadegh. Truman's successor, Eisenhower, was more receptive.

ABOVE: Pro-Mossadegh demonstrators confront soldiers on the streets of the Iranian capital, Teheran, during the vital power struggle that gripped the country in 1953.

RIGHT: Mossadegh at the United Nations, pleading his case. Despite his undoubted popularity in Iran, Mossadegh was doomed once the CIA set to work subverting his government.

during the war and ended up as a Middle East specialist. To carry out the Iran mission he took with him a small band of operatives and a budget of $2 million. They had to operate outside the protection of the US embassy, but local agents were roped in to help them, as were members of Iran's intelligence services.

The plan was to replace Mossadegh by his interior minister General Fazollah Zahedi and at the same time restore the effective power of the Shah. The crisis came in August 1953. Assured of American and

British support, on the 14th the Shah signed a decree dismissing Mossadegh and naming Zahedi as prime minister in his stead. But Mossadegh was confident of his parliamentary and popular support. He arrested the colonel who delivered the decree, declared the Shah's action illegal, and assumed full powers himself. Pro-Mossadegh demonstrations erupted in the streets of Teheran and the Shah fled with his family, first to Baghdad and then on to Rome. There he met CIA Director Allen Dulles who had flown in from the United States. Dulles knew that the situation was far from being lost.

In Teheran, Roosevelt worked frantically to exploit the unstable political balance. Politicians and military leaders were approached and offered various forms of inducement, including straight bribes, to turn against Mossadegh. The text of the Shah's decree was distributed in a vast number of leaflets, and a major counter-demonstration

was organized on the streets of Teheran, previously dominated by the Tudeh and pro-Mossadegh crowds. Roosevelt's activities were outstandingly successful. Mossadegh's supporters lost the initiative and the military leaders primed by the CIA were able to drive him from power after only brief, if bloody, fighting with opposing army elements. Zahedi emerged as the victor and invited the Shah to return from exile.

The overthrow of Mossadegh was, at least in the short term, a triumph for the United States. The following year Western oil companies signed a 25-year agreement with Iran giving US interests a 40 percent share in the country's petroleum. American arms flooded into Iran, US listening bases were established near the Soviet border in the north of the country, and the CIA set about training the Shah's notorious secret police, Savak.

When the Shah and his family (below) were forced to flee Iran in August 1953, they were met in Rome by CIA director Allen Dulles who could assure them that all was not lost. The Shah was soon back on the throne, with full American backing provided by John Foster Dulles (left), US Secretary of State.

Meanwhile, in 1954 the CIA engineered a far more audacious coup considerably nearer home, in the Central American state of Guatemala. It was a horribly poverty-stricken country, in which only two percent of the population owned 70 percent of the land. Over half the people were illiterate and the country was dominated by a single American employer which exploited the workforce, the United Fruit Company: Guatemala was the original 'banana republic.' In 1951 Jacobo Arbenz Guzmán was elected as the country's president. Arbenz was determined to do something for the impoverished population and tried to push through a series of reforms, including

trade union rights for workers and land redistribution. This policy was not welcomed by the United Fruit Company, which had powerful contacts in Washington. At the same time, Arbenz tolerated and co-operated with the Guatemalan communists, although none was included in his cabinet. To the United States, this was intolerable: Arbenz not only threatened US economic dominance but offered a toe-hold to communism in the Americas.

In March 1953 the CIA backed right-wingers in Guatemala with money and arms to stage a revolt, but the rising failed. Eisenhower had decided that 'Arbenz must go', however, so something better would have

Right: Jacobo Arbenz Guzmán, the democratically-elected president of Guatemala, whose reformist policies and tolerance of communist activities were unacceptable to the United States.

to be planned. Although Allen Dulles was nominally in charge, real responsibility for the operation lay with Frank Wisner, Deputy Director of Plans. Wisner chose Guatemalan Colonel Carlos Castillo Armas as the figurehead to lead the planned coup. It was to be presented to the world as a revolt by the Guatemalan military and exiles, without any US involvement. Guatemalan exiles and mercenaries from the United States and South America were assembled at training bases in Nicaragua, an impressive air force of P-47 Thunderbolts and C-47 transports was established at Managua airport, and radio transmitters were set up in Honduras on Guatemala's borders.

In May 1954 the CIA learned of a shipment of arms bound from Czechoslovakia to Guatemala. It was the pretext they needed. Fifty tons of military equipment were shipped from the United States to the training base in Nicaragua and a propaganda campaign magnifying Arbenz' links with communism was mounted in the press throughout Latin America. The United States insisted on the right to search all foreign ships bound for Guatemala. The British refused, and the Dutch and French protested when their ships were searched.

A British official pointed out at the time that America's threatened action against Guatemala amounted to a 'technical act of war'. The official added: 'I have written a private letter to Sir R Makins asking him whether Mr Dulles is going fascist, I can think of no other explanation.'

By June 1954 the combined effect of the propaganda broadcasts from the CIA transmitters in Honduras – the 'Voice of

ABOVE AND TOP: Squalor and malnutrition are the normal lot of the Guatemalan poor, housed in shanty towns and reduced to picking over trash. President Arbenz sought to change this state of affairs.

Liberation' operated by David Phillips – and the aggressive campaign of accusations against Arbenz started to gain effect. Arbenz grounded the air force, suspecting it of disloyalty, and the air force commander defected to the CIA-backed side. At a meeting in Washington shortly before the planned invasion, Eisenhower asked whether the operation would succeed. Apparently in answer to his own question, Eisenhower said: 'I'm prepared to take any steps that are necessary to see that [this mission] succeeds. For if it succeeds, it's the people of Guatemala throwing off the yoke of communism. If it fails the flag of the United States has failed.' This was said despite the fact that Arbenz had been democratically elected by the Guatemalan people.

On June 18 Castillo Armas and his 'Army of Liberation' crossed the border into Guatemala from Honduras. On the same day the P-47s bombed San Jose, a major Guatemalan port on the Pacific coast. The invasion was magnified by the activities of David Phillips and the 'Voice of Liberation';

Phillips fabricated whole news broadcasts, listing battles and defeats which were pure figments of his imagination, yet the demoralizing effect these broadcasts must have had on listening Guatemalans cannot be overestimated. Simultaneously leaflet raids were being carried out over Guatemala City, interspersed with bombing attacks. Guatemala accused the United States in the UN of being actively involved in these raids, a charge which the Americans repudiated, claiming that 'the situation does not involve aggression but is a revolt of Guatemalans against Guatemalans'. Allen Dulles, meanwhile, had successfully requisitioned further planes through President Eisenhower. The acquisition of the planes was laundered through certain dubious payments made by Nicaragua. By 27 June the strain had proved too much for Arbenz and he handed over to Colonel Carlos Diaz, head of the Guatemalan armed forces. To the horror of the CIA, however, Diaz declared his intention of fighting the rebel invaders. Further bombing raids were launched against Guatemala

BELOW: Arbenz (second from left) with his wife and government ministers at a public ceremony some time before the president's overthrow. The strain of staying in power in the face of continuous CIA-inspired conspiracies is clearly visible in their faces.

LEFT: Colonel Carlos Castillo Armas, the leader of the CIA-backed invasion of Guatemala and successor to Arbenz as president. One of his first acts on taking power was to disenfranchize 70 percent of the population, although the Eisenhower Administration represented his takeover as a triumph for democracy.

City, and this time the headquarters of the Guatemalan Army was hit. Diaz, president for a day, was ousted and a new junta formed. On 2 July a pact was signed between Castillo Armas and the junta, which eventually led to Castillo Armas assuming the presidency. There followed a lengthy reign of terror for the Guatemalan people. In one foul swoop 70 percent of the Guatemalan population was disenfranchised by an act which denied illiterates the vote. Labor and union rights were repealed and 800,000 acres of land was taken from the peasants and handed back to the United Fruit Company.

Talking about Guatemala on US television Foster Dulles said: 'the struggle in Guatemala exposed the evil purpose of the Kremlin to find nesting places in the Americas.' He added: 'Led by Colonel Castillo Armas, patriots arose in Guatemala to challenge the communist leadership and to change it. Thus the situation is being cured by the Guatemalans themselves.' It later transpired that the whole operation had cost the CIA $20 million.

Cuba was another country with which the United States became involved; indeed, for a time the affairs of that country were to dominate US foreign policy. In November 1956 Fidel Castro landed on Cuba with 81 followers bent on overthrowing the dictatorship of Fulgencio Batista. By 1959, against all odds, the rebels had succeeded and Castro was able to establish his own regime. At first the Americans were not hostile to the new government, but they soon became so when Castro declared his intention of supporting guerrilla movements against US-backed dictatorships throughout Latin America and seized US assets in Cuba. He also established friendly relations with the Soviet Union, although he was not himself a communist.

In December 1959 Colonel J C King, head of the CIA's Western Hemisphere Division, wrote to Allen Dulles expressing his fears for the area as a whole. Cuba, it was well noted, was only 90 miles from the United States itself. King recommended that 'thorough consideration be given to the elimination of Fidel Castro – the disappearance of Fidel would greatly accelerate the fall of the present government.' Dulles approved of this recommendation and a meeting of the National Security Council was held, at which it was agreed to create a Special Group to look into any possible action against Cuba. After further meetings of this Special Group, a CIA Task Force was set up to carry out its wishes, including the creation of an armed force of Cuban exiles, an attempt to form a subversive organization inside Cuba, and if possible the assassination of Castro.

Eisenhower was aware of the plans to eliminate Castro. In his memoirs he says: 'On 17 March 1960, I ordered the CIA to begin to organize the training of Cuban exiles mainly in Guatemala against a future day when they might return to their homeland.' Eisenhower had also been in attendance at the National Security Council meetings where the proposals to murder Castro were raised. Castro's two major colleagues, Che Guevara and brother Raúl Castro, were also to be 'eliminated.'

The initial plan was to discredit Castro in front of his nation. Castro had an immense following within Cuba. He was charismatic

BELOW: President Fulgencio Batista of Cuba wreathed in smiles, having just escaped an assassination attempt in March 1957. Batista's days as dictator of Cuba were already numbered, however, as Fidel Castro had begun his guerrilla campaign on the island the previous November.

Fidel Castro, as guerrilla leader (below) and as national leader and world statesman (left). Castro's victory in Cuba at the start of 1959 initially met with an uncertain response from the United States, but when he started to export revolution to the rest of Latin America and established friendly relations with the Soviet Union, the CIA decided he had to be got rid of.

and he had successfully rid the country of a hated dictatorship; therefore, the CIA planned to wage a war of dirty tricks against him, designed to show Cuba that Castro was indeed fallible and also could look extremely silly. The ideas that the Agency came up with were comic, to say the least. The first was to spray Cuban TV studios with LSD (the Agency had been experimenting with the drug for some time) prior to Castro broadcasting a speech, the idea being that Castro would behave absurdly and appear a complete buffoon. The plan was abandoned since no one could guarantee that the experiment would have the desired effect. The second idea was to doctor Castro's famous insignia – his cigars. This scheme was also abandoned when the Agency could not work out how to get the cigars to Castro. Another in this crazy chain of ideas was to make Castro's beard fall out. Scientists knew that thallium salts, when in contact with skin, would act as a depilatory. They reasoned that if Castro were to travel and leave his shoes outside the hotel bedroom, the salts could be sprinkled in his boots. This number collapsed when Castro cancelled all forthcoming foreign trips. It is amazing that an Agency which prided itself on being professional and above all intelligent could actually believe that any of these plots could have worked.

Despite this buffoonery the Agency was still pursuing its more serious plans for

On 14 October 1962 a U2 reconnaissance flight over Cuba, gathering intelligence on the Soviet military aid arriving for Fidel Castro, brought back photos showing preparations for a medium-range ballistic missile base at San Cristóbal. The idea that Soviet nuclear missiles might be stationed so close to the United States was totally unacceptable to the Kennedy administration. Rejecting calls from the Joint Chiefs of Staff for an invasion of Cuba or air strikes, President Kennedy ordered a naval blockade to turn back any vessels carrying Soviet war materials and warned that if the build-up continued, war would follow. On 28 October Soviet premier Nikita Khrushchev finally agreed to dismantle the missile sites, on condition that the United States promised not to invade Cuba. For Kennedy, brinkmanship had worked.

TOP: Cuban leader Fidel Castro (left) on a visit to Moscow, alongside Soviet premier Nikita Krushchev. The close relationship between Cuba and the Soviet Union worried the United States even before Soviet arms began to pour into the island. ABOVE: A Soviet vessel bound for Cuba with a cargo of Il-28 bombers. RIGHT: A U2 photo of Soviet missiles in Cuba — the sort of evidence, provided by the CIA, that provoked the crisis.

LAUNCH STANDS

17 MISSILE ERECTORS

MISSILE READY TENT FOUNDATIONS (TENTS REMOVED)

ABANDONED LAUNCH POSITION

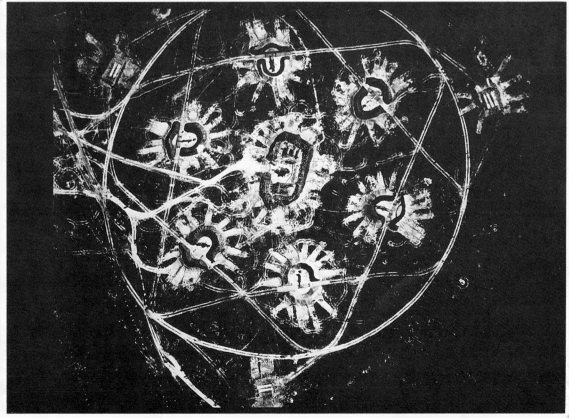

ABOVE: An aerial photo taken on 1 November 1962 reveals the Soviets dismantling their medium range ballistic missile site at San Cristóbal, marking the end of the confrontation with the United States. LEFT: An SA 2 missile site on Cuba. The CIA's intelligence performance during the crisis was markedly more successful than its covert operations against Castro's regime.

eliminating Castro. In July 1960 a Cuban agent reported that he was shortly to have access to Raúl Castro, Fidel's brother. The CIA back in the United States was delighted and immediately briefed its man in Cuba to carry out an assassination. At the last minute, though, plans were changed and the agent's instructions were rescinded. The need to destroy Castro consumed the Agency to the extent that they approached the Mafia to take charge of matters for them. To do this Robert Maheu, a former FBI agent, was employed. Through a long chain of command Maheu's authorization can be traced right back to Deputy Director of Plans Richard Bissell. Maheu had been actively employed by the CIA before when he had produced a pornographic movie which had been doctored to show Indonesia's President Sukarno in very compromising situations. The aim of the film had been to discredit Sukarno and demonstrate that he was a complete Soviet puppet.

Maheu hired John Rosselli, a powerful Las Vegas-based Mafia Boss at a fee of $150,000 to assassinate Castro. Maheu told Rosselli he would be doing a great service for his country and also invented the cover story that behind the plot were wealthy Americans who wanted to recover their seized Havana assets. Rosselli soon gathered who was really behind it but still agreed to carry out the work. Rosselli embroiled two of America's most wanted men in the plot, Sam Giancana, chief US Mafia boss, and Santos Trafficante, Cuba Mafia chief. The CIA liaison man, Chief of Operational Support Division James O'Connell, met these men and immediately recognized them. While the CIA was not too fussy about using known gangland figures for its devious activities, the FBI objected strongly and was furious that it could not arrest the Mafia men.

US Mafia boss Sam Giancana (right) was recruited by the CIA in its labyrinthine plots to assassinate or discredit Castro. Another of the targets for assassination was Castro's young Argentinian-born comrade-in-arms Ernesto 'Che' Guevara (below). None of the CIA's mostly farcical plans came anywhere near succeeding.

The Mafia were largely involved in further attempts to poison Castro. By using a contact who worked in a Cuban restaurant where Castro frequently dined, the Agency hoped to doctor Castro's food with the poison botulinum toxin, a known killer. This attempt also floundered: some accounts say that Castro stopped using the restaurant, others suggest the unlikely theory that the CIA did not finally authorize the operation. Plots to assassinate Castro continued to be floated up to 1965.

Meanwhile, in November 1960 John F Kennedy was elected President. By that time the development of the Cuban exile force was already well advanced. Eisenhower had approved a $13 million budget for the program the previous August and a force of some 1300 men had been assembled and trained. Cuban pilots were being shown how to fly B-26 bombers by Alabama

National Guardsmen recruited for the job. Many of those behind the Guatemalan coup were again involved, including David Phillips, the radio propaganda expert, who set up a broadcasting station on Swan Island, off Honduras. Codenamed JM/WAVE, the whole operation was controlled and planned from the campus of the University of Miami. Print shops, gun shops, coffee shops and other cover establishments were founded in Florida to give the CIA a screen behind which it could operate. Obviously, though, such a massive operation could not take place without attracting public notice; Castro himself talked about the American plans to overthrow him.

As the date for the invasion approached, uncertainty about the CIA plans grew. Richard Bissel, Deputy Director of Plans, had responsibility for it, but his second-in-command, Richard Helms, would have nothing to do with the scheme. The CIA's own intelligence reports showed that the popular uprising that was supposed to greet the exile landings was very unlikely to occur. The US Joint Chiefs of Staff were unimpressed by the CIA's planning, and Kennedy was extremely nervous about any direct US involvement. In a series of com-promises designed to cut down on US support for the Cuban exiles, the amount of air cover was reduced and the landings were shifted from a more favourable site to the Bay of Pigs, where it was felt the landing force could get ashore with a minimum of naval and air force back-up.

Escorted by US naval vessels, the 1300-strong invasion force crossed to Cuba and landed on 17 April 1961. Air attacks by the

LEFT: Richard Helms, a future director of the CIA, distanced himself from the Agency's plans for an invasion of Cuba, which ended in the Bay of Pigs fiasco of April 1961.

BELOW: A member of the Cuban exile invasion force at the Bay of Pigs is interrogated by Castro's soldiers. About 1180 of the invaders were taken prisoner, the other 120 losing their lives in the fighting.

six B-26s now assigned to the operation were inadequate, however, and the expected support from opponents of the regime organized by agents inside Cuba never materialized. Hopelessly exposed to counterattacks by the Cuban air force and tanks, the whole of the invasion force was either killed or taken prisoner, and Castro's regime rose to new heights of popularity.

Although a wavering political leadership

RIGHT: John A McCone, who replaced Allen Dulles as head of the CIA after the Bay of Pigs episode. The plots to assassinate Castro continued under McCone.

BELOW: The CIA headquarters at Langley, Virginia, a large and expensive complex of buildings, but very discreetly located.

contributed as much as the CIA to the Bay of Pigs debacle, a shake-up of the Agency followed. Dulles was made the scapegoat: in November 1961 he was replaced as head of the Agency by a Kennedy appointee, John A McCone. But there was no question of running down the CIA. It was at this stage that the Agency moved to its present headquarters in Langley, Virginia. Set in rolling woodland the headquarters is virtually invisible to the peering eyes of strangers; it was funded by $46 million from Congress and over its main entrance doors has enscribed: 'And ye shall know the truth and the truth shall make you free.'

The Bay of Pigs Affair was not the final note in this extraordinarily controversial tune. The Soviets decided that Cuba's proximity to the United States could provide them with a very useful missile base, so in 1962 scores of Soviet technicians moved to Cuba. At first they started to ship in SA-2 anti-aircraft missiles and other SA-2 short-range defensive missiles. These the United States discovered through CIA-organized U2 spying missions over Cuba. But further flights over Cuba revealed that mobile medium-range ballistic missile sites were also being constructed. These could be used for offensive operations against the US mainland. On 22 October, after a fortnight of intensive meetings between the White

House, the National Security Council and the CIA, the President announced on American television that due to the discovery of the missiles the United States was to impose a blockade around Cuba. Kennedy added that the blockade would be the first step and that if Cuba did not dismantle the missiles direct military action might have to be considered. Tension between the two superpowers was high, and the world believed that a major war was liable to break out at any time. On 26 October Khrushchev signalled that he was prepared to dismantle the missiles under UN supervision in return for two promises: the first was that the United States would lift the blockade and the second was that the United States would never invade Cuba. Kennedy accepted these proposals and the Soviets eventually started to dismantle the missiles.

It is perhaps interesting that this coup on behalf of the United States had taken place through overt diplomatic channels, apart from the initial CIA detection of the missile sites. This contrasts starkly with the total failure of all forms of covert action.

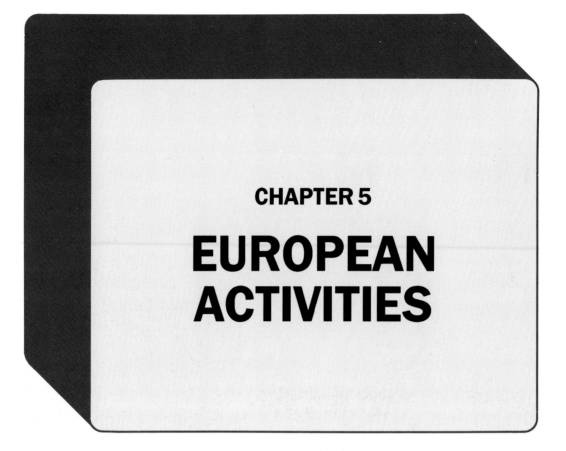

CHAPTER 5

EUROPEAN ACTIVITIES

The CIA and the KGB may dominate the world of espionage but that does not mean to say that other countries have not retained their own networks, though increasingly in terms of manpower and finance these other agencies are having to rely on the might and power of the two world superpowers.

One of the areas where this mutual dependency is highlighted is the so-called 'special relationship' between the United States and Britain, which among other things allows shared global eavesdropping facilities at the Government Communications Headquarters (GCHQ) based in Cheltenham, England. In 1947 a secret treaty known as UKUSA was signed to link the US National Security Agency (NSA) with GCHQ. This agreement allows the two to have access to intercept messages and communications from all over the world. Similar treaties exist between Australia, Canada, New Zealand and all Nato countries. As well as having earth-based

listening posts the United States has used its space program for 'piggy-backing' numerous spy satellites into space. These satellites are estimated to be so strong that they can pick up conversations between Soviet officials using their car-telephones. The GCHQ Hong Kong base was responsible for providing the US with valuable information during the Vietnam War.

GCHQ also operates in a domestic capacity carrying out telephone tapping and computer encryption on behalf of the British internal security service, MI5. It was a team of scientists at the Joint Technical Language Services (JTLS) unit from GCHQ who devised the 'key word' method of telephone tapping, a process whereby if a sensitive word is used over a telephone line which is monitored, then that conversation will be tapped. In Britain the main domestic tapping center is based at Chantrey House in Victoria, London. It is also believed that a far larger capacity exists for the tapping of

ABOVE AND LEFT: GCHQ, Cheltenham, England. The dull modern building gives nothing away, but the huge radio receivers reveal the purpose of one of the world's most sophisticated espionage centers. Used by both Britain and the United States, GCHQ can listen in to conversations across Europe, even picking up the gossip of Moscow taxi drivers.

international lines at a City address, also in London. The NSA has a UK base in Menwith Hill, Yorkshire. Some experts believe that Menwith Hill is the biggest tapping facility in the world, far larger than anything the KGB can muster. Menwith Hill is also connected to Britain's own telecommunications lines; in the late 1970s an American NSA analyst confirmed that Menwith Hill has the 'authority for tapping all telephone lines to Europe.'

Britain's image was tarnished in 1982 when a KGB spy, Geoffrey Prime, was charged with espionage. Prime had worked at GCHQ and it is believed that he had been passing secrets to the Soviets since 1968. Prime was caught by a sheer fluke, not through any sophisticated detection by British security agencies. Prime had left GCHQ in 1977 and since that time had had only two contacts with his Soviet paymasters, one in 1980 in Vienna and the other in 1981 in Berlin. His unmasking came about when he was arrested by local police on charges of pederasty. Prime's wife Rhona, who had only recently found out

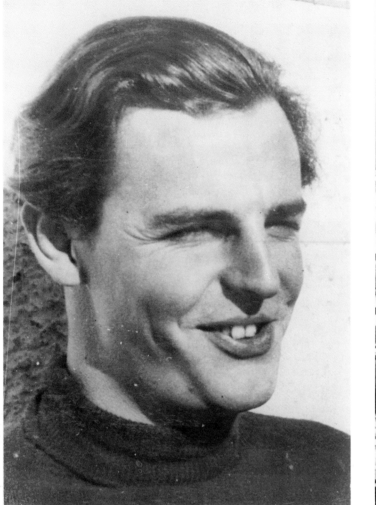

Donald Maclean (above) and Guy Burgess (above right) created a sensation in May 1951 when they defected to the Soviet Union. American sources believe that, although the pair were tipped off by Philby, they would still have been caught if the British secret services had been prepared to work at the weekend; instead of pulling them in on a Friday evening, MI5 decided to leave it until the following Monday, by which time they had disappeared to the Continent.

about Prime's sexual activities, decided to inform the police about his previous secret life. The Prime affair severely strained relations between Britain and the United States: the Americans referred to Cheltenham as being 'as leaky as an old sow'. It is difficult to assess what damage Prime actually caused, given that his trial was held 'in camera,' but expert observers believe he revealed secrets related to a project dubbed 'Byeman,' a new surveillance system consisting of powerful satellites which could pick up all the details the West could want about the activities of the Soviet Union. A further project which Prime possibly revealed was the top secret Argus satellite, launched in June 1975. Argus could detect voice transmissions with such clarity that conversations between Warsaw Pact tank commanders could be picked up. Prime's information gave the KGB vital knowledge about NSA/GCHQ computers and their awesome capacity; it also allowed the Soviets to gain a complete picture of the Allied spy satellite program. It is no wonder that the NSA was furious with Britain once the enormity of Prime's crime had been revealed.

Of course, Geoffrey Prime was far from being the first KGB spy to have been unmasked in Britain. Nuclear scientists Alan Nunn May and Klaus Fuchs were arrested for passing atomic secrets to the Soviets in 1946 and 1950 respectively. But the revelation of their deeds was as nothing compared with the Burgess and Maclean affair that broke in 1951, almost totally destroying American confidence in the British security services. The defection of the two men to Moscow caused a sensation. But the true scale of the penetration of MI6 was not publicly known for many years.

Motivated by a belief in communism widespread amongst the British intelligentsia of the 1930s, a group of young men at Cambridge University had become involved with the Soviet spy service. As well as Donald Maclean and Guy Burgess, there was Kim Philby and the slightly older Anthony Blunt, who acted as a talent spotter for the Soviets. During World War II all of them achieved positions in the British secret or diplomatic services, Blunt with MI5, Philby in MI6 and the others in related operations. Blunt left the spy world in 1945, having passed a considerable amount of information to the Soviet Union during the war years. Burgess, a chronic drunk and

flagrant homosexual, never achieved a position of any trust. But Maclean and Philby progressed well in their chosen profession. Maclean became First Secretary at the British Embassy in Washington and was appointed as Britain's representative to the Combined Policy Committee for Joint Atomic Development. He soon had the run of the US Atomic Energy Commission building. Meanwhile Philby, a highly intelligent man (and the only one of the Cambridge group not a homosexual) had risen to the top of MI6's counter-espionage section and been appointed to liaise with the CIA in Washington. We have already seen the effect Philby's betrayal had on joint CIA/MI6 operations in Eastern Europe (see chapter 2).

The CIA's James Angleton was suspicious of both Philby and Maclean. The Americans revealed their suspicions about Maclean to the British and he was withdrawn to London. By May 1951, the net was closing around Maclean, but Philby was well placed to save him. Through Burgess and Blunt – drawn out of his retirement from spying – Maclean was tipped off that he was about to be pulled in for interrogation. As the plan for Maclean's disappearance was

set in motion, Burgess insisted on going along with him. The pair left ostensibly for a short holiday on the Continent and only resurfaced in Moscow.

The finger now pointed at Philby, especially as Burgess had been staying with him in the United States just before the defection. The Americans refused to work with Philby any longer, but MI6 found it hard to believe in his guilt. He stood up well under interrogation, showing all his strength of character and intelligence. However, Philby was eased out of MI6 by degrees, and by 1963 when he finally defected to Moscow, he was only loosely associated with the service in a 'freelance' capacity. Philby's career did not end with his defection; he reportedly became an important advisor to Yuri Andropov, head of the KGB and later leader of the Soviet Union.

Another MI6 double agent who did immense damage at a lower level in the service was George Blake. Before his arrest in 1961, Blake had spied for the KGB for 10 years, apparently having been converted to communism during a spell in a North Korean prisoner-of-war camp in 1951. Sentenced to 42 years in prison, Blake made a spectacular escape from Wormwood

Anthony Blunt (above left) was the last of the four Cambridge spies to be exposed. His close relationship with the Queen made his treachery especially shocking to the British establishment. 'Kim' Philby (above) also disarmed suspicion because of his upper-class background, and through his diligence and efficiency as a member of MI6.

RIGHT: Yuri Andropov, head of the KGB and subsequently Soviet leader. Philby reportedly acted as one of Andropov's most trusted advisors after defecting to Moscow.

BELOW: Soviet newspaper *Isvestia* welcomes Philby to the Soviet Union in 1963, when he finally defected via Beirut after living under suspicion in the West for a decade. The headline reads: 'Hello, Comrade Philby.'

Scrubs in October 1966 and later surfaced in Moscow – yet another embarrassment for Britain.

If former MI5 man Peter Wright is to be believed, US distrust of the British security services had reached such a level in 1965 that the CIA carried out a clandestine examination of MI5, MI6 and GCHQ. The conclusion of their report was, apparently, almost entirely negative – as far as the CIA was concerned, the British could not be trusted.

Outside the intelligence services themselves, perhaps the most famous spy case in Britain was the so-called 'Portland Spy Ring.' This was an offshoot of Rudolf Abel's network in the United States. Morris and Lona Cohen, two American communists who had been contacted by Abel in New York, left for London by a very circuitous route in 1950 – via Canada, Singapore, the Soviet Union, Austria, and France – picking up the birth certificates of a dead New Zealand couple, Peter and Helen Kroger, in Paris. With these documents they obtained a New Zealand passport and entered Britain

ЗДРАВСТВУЙТЕ, ТОВАРИЩ ФИЛБИ

«Если бы мне предстояло начать жизнь сызнова, я начал бы так, как начал».

Феликс ДЗЕРЖИНСКИЙ.

ДЕКАБРЬСКОЕ морозное утро, ночная мгла еще не ушла с заснеженных улиц. Деревья на Гоголевском бульваре покрыты пушистым инеем. У троллейбусной остановки — цепочка потирающих щеки, приплясывающих москвичей. Начинается новый день с его заботами, суетой. Автомобили тоже торопятся, обгоняют друг друга.

Среднего роста невысокий, но крепкий еще человек неторопливо шагает по тротуару, с удовольствием вдыхая морозный воздух. На нем теплое, подбитое цигейкой пальто, меховая шапка. Человек откровенно радуется и этому утру, и морозу, и бурному потоку пешеходов. Его иногда толкают. «Простите, — торопливо извиняется он, «ничего», — приветливо говорит он, говорит с легким акцентом.

Кто он, этот человек? Чему он улыбается, что необыкновенного нашел он в бульваре, запорошенных деревьях, в этом обычном московском утре?

Его называли человеком-загадкой, жизнь его ребус? Долгие годы, целые десятилетия, тридцать лет бесконечных загадок. Жизнь сложная, как лабиринт.

ВЕСЕННИМ утром 1951 года в кабинете одного из руководителей Центрального разведывательного управления, святая святых американской секретной службы, было созвано важное совещание. Кроме Аллена Даллеса, за длинным полированным столом сидел Фрэнк Уизнер, руководитель службы по проведению сверхсекретных подрывных политических операций.

представить все, что угодно. Предположить, что в то августовское утро в кабинете за столом напротив него сидел кадровый сотрудник советской разведки, он не мог даже в дурном сне.

Советский разведчик Ким Филби очередное задание центра выполнил.

И ВОТ настала наша очередь сесть за один стол с Кимом Филби. Стол невелик, не блещет полировкой. Заваленный бумагами старинной работы английский стол.

— Начнем с начала, — мягко предлагает он, — от печки, как говорят по-русски.

Его английский выдает в нем человека высокой культуры.

Он родился в индийском городке Амбала и провел в Индии первые четыре года своей жизни.

— Первого января мне исполнится 56, — рассказывает Ким Филби. — Мой отец служил чиновником английской колониальной администрации в Индии.

— А что за странное имя Ким вам дали?

— Я делал, что мог в то время, и был счастлив узнать однажды, что я зачислен в кадры советской разведки.

— Каким же образом, товарищ Ким, вам удалось попасть на службу в английскую разведку?

— Это довольно длинная история, — говорит он. — После окончания Кэмбриджа я некоторое время работал в одной редакции, а затем отправился военным корреспондентом в Испанию от газеты «Таймс». Шел февраль 1937 года.

— Я пошел вверх по служебной лестнице. Через год я уже был заместителем начальника одного из отделов МИ-6.

— МИ-6, что это значит?

— В Англии существует две службы: под названием МИ-5 скрывается контрразведка. МИ-6 — собственно секретная разведывательная служба.

— Товарищ Ким, западная пресса утверждает, что вы были третьим по важности лицом в британской секретной службе.

— Я справлялся со своими обязанностями, мною были довольны. В 1946 году меня наградили Орденом Британской Империи.

with the greatest of ease. There they were joined by another Soviet agent, Konon Trofimovich Molody, better known as Gordon Lonsdale, who had also worked for Abel. Lonsdale and the Krogers ran a spy ring from 1956 until 1961, particularly in connection with Harry Houghton, an Englishman working at the Underwater Weapons Establishment, Portland. Lonsdale and the Krogers were exposed, along with Blake, in 1961 when Soviet agent Anatoli Golitsyn defected to the West. They only served short terms of imprisonment before being 'spy-swapped' to the Soviet Union.

It has been suggested that the reason for the success of such spies as Lonsdale and Philby was partly the presence of a double agent at the head of MI5, Sir Roger Hollis. From 1956 to 1965, it is alleged, Hollis protected Philby, Blunt (who was never prosecuted although his treachery was known), and Lonsdale, among others. However, the allegations against Hollis may have emanated from MI6, an example of the endless infighting between the two services. By

LEFT: George Blake. Although not as high level a double agent as Philby, Blake passed secrets to the Soviets for almost a decade before his arrest in 1961.

BELOW: The house in the London suburbs where Soviet spies Morris and Lona Cohen, better known under their alias as Peter and Helen Kroger, ran the 'Portland Spy Ring.' Their cover was an innocent-seeming antiquarian bookshop.

In-fighting between MI5 and MI6 has long been a feature of British secret service life. Sir Roger Hollis (above), one-time head of MI5, has been denounced as a Soviet agent, because of rumors put about by MI6. Sir Maurice Oldfield (above right) former head of MI6, had his homosexual past exposed by MI5.

RIGHT: Gordon Lonsdale, who posed as a respectable businessman while in fact spying for the KGB in Britain as an associate of the Krogers. Arrested in 1961, Lonsdale was spy-swapped back to the Soviet Union in 1964.

the same token, revelations that Sir Maurice Oldfield, head of MI6 from 1974 to 1978, had a murky homosexual past may well have originated with MI5, angered by Oldfield's appointment as security co-ordinator for Northern Ireland in 1979, which they considered their own preserve. At times, secret services seem to spend more effort fighting their own allies than their enemies – a charge that merits serious consideration.

The failings of British security have often led to calls for greater openness and parliamentary control. Officially MI6 does not even exist, although bus conductors on the route which leads past the MI6 headquarters at Century House, Westminster Bridge Road, always refer to that bus stop as 'spooks stop' ('spooks' is slang for spies). Compared to the CIA, MI6 is notoriously secretive. At least since the mid-1970s, the American people have considerable knowledge about the CIA, but MI6 is protected by the draconian Official Secrets Act. Expenditure and activities of MI6 never come before the British parliament: it has been estimated that the combined budgets for MI6, MI5 and GCHQ amount to over £40 million a year but this could well be a very low estimate.

LEFT: This door in Queen Anne's Gate, London, leads into the hidden world of MI6. Yet although the addresses of the secret service's main buildings in London are public knowledge, officially its very existence is denied.

THE BERLIN WALL

On 13 August 1961, in the early hours of the morning, East Berlin was sealed off from the West by a barrier of barbed wire and fencing, soon to be replaced by more permanent concrete. The Wall blocked the last remaining point of free movement between Eastern and Western Europe, through which some 150,000 East Germans had been passing each year, in search of better-paid jobs, better living conditions, and greater political and cultural freedom. The blocking of movement between East and West Berlin also stopped the easiest espionage route in Europe, and in particular made it more difficult for both East and West German secret services to plant agents in their enemy's camp. But Berlin remained a great spy center, with the traditional location for spy swaps at the Glienecker Bridge checkpoint.

BELOW: East Berlin border guards look out from the Wall into the West.

LEFT, BELOW, AND BOTTOM: Slicing across the middle of the city, splitting not only streets but also families and friends, the Berlin Wall has become the symbol of a divided Europe.

ABOVE: Journalists visit a tunnel under the Soviet sector of Berlin, dug by Western intelligence services to eavesdrop on Soviet communications but uncovered in 1956. The unique position of Berlin as a meeting-point of East and West made it the classic location for infiltration of enemy services, recruiting of double agents, and spy swaps.

An example of a successful operation brought about by one of the smaller intelligence agencies is offered by the Polish intelligence agency, the UB, between 1951 and 1967. In 1951 a concentration camp survivor by the name of Linowsky, now living in West Germany, was recruited by the UB while visiting relatives in Poland. He in turn recruited two West Germans, Manfred Ramminger and Wolf Knoppe, the latter a pilot at the West German airbase of Zell. Aided by Knoppe, Linowsky was able to penetrate the airbase and steal a Litton LM-II navigation box. Linowsky's next instructions were to steal a Phantom aircraft, but possibly realizing the difficulty of such an exploit, he decided instead to steal a Sidewinder AIM-9E air-to-air guided missile. Knoppe helped out again by giving Linowsky his base security pass and also identified the Sidewinder storage shed. The two men then successfully stole the missile and walked out of the base carrying it. Once

RIGHT: Hans Clemens, one of the ex-SS men recruited by West German intelligence who also spied for the Russians.

BELOW: Manfred Ramminger, who helped steal a Sidewinder missile from West Germany.

outside, the missile was loaded into a car and taken to an apartment 200 miles away on the other side of West Germany. It was then dismantled and packed into crates, labelled 'business samples,' and the crates were driven to Düsseldorf airport from where they were flown to Moscow via Copenhagen. Ramminger boarded the same plane but to his horror, upon disembarkation in Moscow, he discovered that the precious cargo had not arrived. A

zealous bureaucrat had had the crates returned to Düsseldorf to be properly labelled. Ramminger went back to Düsseldorf, redeemed his cargo and then put it and himself on the next plane to the Soviet Union. Eventually the West Germans caught up with the trio and they were sentenced to short terms of imprisonment. Ramminger was released early and exchanged for Western spies in 1971.

Germany was a natural center for spying activities, because of the special circumstances created by the division of the country between the Soviet and Western powers in 1945. Berlin, with its Western sectors isolated in the middle of communist territory, has been the site not only of numerous spy-swaps, but also of such spectacular espionage efforts as the CIA's digging of a tunnel under the Eastern sector

LEFT: Reinhard Gehlen in his Nazi guise, before the CIA turned him into a defender of Western democracy.

ABOVE: Hans-Joachim Tiedge, one of the many East German double agents planted successfully in the West.

to eavesdrop on East German telephone communications. The two Germanys found it relatively easy to infiltrate 'moles' into one another's security services or government organizations and double agents were more common than elsewhere.

The West German intelligence agency grew out of a group founded after the war by the ex-Nazi Reinhard Gehlen, funded by the CIA. Gehlen had belonged to Hitler's wartime intelligence for Foreign Armies East, controlling the Nazi's East European intelligence network. In 1945 Gehlen surrendered both himself and his valuable files to the US Counter Intelligence Corps. The CIA realized that in Gehlen they had discovered someone whose knowledge was likely to prove invaluable, and because of this they were prepared to overlook his wartime activities and allow him to establish his own intelligence agency in West Germany. Gehlen then set about recruiting old wartime buddies, many of whom had been in the SS. In July 1950 the Bonn administration announced that it was to take over the Gehlen organization, which was to be renamed the Bundesnachrichtendienst (Federal News Service – BND). Gehlen still remained in charge and managed some intelligence coups, notably installing one of his agents, Ernst Gramsch, near the top of East German intelligence. But BND was also penetrated by the East Germans.

In 1963 there was a public scandal when three West German agents, Hans Clemens, Erwin Tiebel and Heinz Felfe, were convicted of spying for the Soviet Union. All of them had been members of the Swiss department of the Nazi Reich Security Service during the war and had been recruited by Gehlen. Felfe, as head of BND counter-espionage, is thought to have done untold damage. Between them, the three men had delivered 15,000 photographs of West German intelligence files and spools of tape recordings to Soviet agents in East Berlin. It was not until this trial that the West German and American publics became aware that Gehlen had such a murky past and they had some difficulty understanding how this man had gained such a high position and been allowed to hire ex-Nazis, including former SS men, with which to staff his intelligence organization.

The East German equivalent to the BND, the Hauptverwaltung Aufklärung (HVA), achieved its greatest success when one of its agents, Gunther Guillaume, was established as a confidential aide in the office of West German Chancellor Willy Brandt. The arrest of Guillaume in April 1974 led to

ABOVE: Liao Ho-shu, a Chinese diplomat in the Netherlands, seeks asylum in the West. Liao revealed details of the workings of the Chinese secret service in Europe, including a 1966 murder in The Hague.

Brandt's resignation and a political crisis in West Germany. It was the outstanding example of the security problems that both Germanys have to endure.

As well as the activities of the European agencies, in the 1960s China was also involved in spy incidents in Europe. In 1966 a Chinese man was found on the streets of the Hague outside the Chinese legation. The man, who was alive but in great pain, was Hsu Tsu-tsai, allegedly a member of a visiting delegation of the International Institute of Welding. The members of the legation

claimed that Hsu had fallen out of a window and allowed him to be taken to a nearby hospital for treatment for a fractured skull, spinal injuries and fractured ribs. Two members of the legation accompanied Hsu to the hospital where, as soon as he was unattended on a trolley, he was snatched back. The Dutch foreign ministry was furious and demanded that Hsu be returned to hospital for treatment. Nothing happened and several days later the Chinese announced that Hsu had died from his injuries. The Dutch demanded an autopsy on Hsu's body, where it was revealed that the unfortunate man had met an exceedingly violent death. The Dutch declared the Chinese chargé d'affaires *persona non grata* and threatened to arrest anyone who left the legation. Peking announced its intention to retaliate in exactly the same way. Eventually the two sides agreed to differ and the Dutch chargé d'affaires was allowed to return home, as were the Chinese.

In 1969 yet another bizarre incident concerning the Chinese and the Hague occurred. On 24 January a pajama-clad Chinese walked into the Hague police station and demanded political asylum. The man was Liao Ho-shu, the Chinese chargé d'affaires and the man who had been responsible for Hsu's hospital abduction. Liao was flown to the United States where the reasons for Hsu's mysterious death were revealed. Hsu had in fact been working for the CIA. His comrades not in fact welders but members of the Chinese intelligence organization, had discovered his betrayal and had murdered him. The murder had taken place when Hsu was on his way to meet his CIA contact. The 'delegates' had signalled to a waiting car to chase Hsu which it did at very high speed, knocking him down and killing him. Liao had probably defected in response to investigations from Peking realizing that his return home could only lead to imprisonment or death.

The final act of the spy game in Europe in the 1960s came in 1969 when Josef Frolik defected from the Czech secret service. When he first arrived in the West he was hailed as a 'big catch,' a very important spy with access to a mass of secret information. On closer examination, however, it was found that a lot of the information that he brought with him just did not make sense. A lot of his information related to the activities of the British Labour Party and the alleged penetration of communists into British trade unions. He named Will Owen, a Labour MP, as having been involved with the Czech Secret Service. Owen was tried in 1970 and

found not guilty. Frolik also named another Labour MP, John Stonehouse, as a KGB agent. John Stonehouse did mysteriously disappear in 1974 and eventually turned up in Australia after his family and friends had believed him to be dead. He then returned to Britain and went to prison for deception; the matter of him possibly belonging to the KGB was not raised. Frolik went on to write a book, entitled *The Frolik Defection*, in which he hinted at murky deeds but refused to name any of the alleged spies. Frolik's allegations were investigated under the Wilson government of 1974-76 and to date they have proved groundless.

Possibly because the great battles for Europe had already been fought, or possibly because the superpower agencies already controlled so much European information-gathering, the period of the 1960s in Europe seems low-key in comparison with the myriad of spy battles that were being fought in Africa and the Middle East. This is the area where vicious battles were being fought, some of which continue to the present day.

ABOVE: Labour MP John Stonehouse was denounced by Czech defector Josef Frolik as a Soviet agent. Yet it would appear that Stonehouse's mysterious 'disappearance' in 1974 was unconnected with espionage.

CHAPTER 6

STRUGGLE FOR THE THIRD WORLD

One of the CIA's first forays into Africa was the Agency's audacious attempt to assassinate Patrice Lumumba, prime minister of the newly independent state of the Congo (now Zaire). In June 1960 the Congo had been granted independence by the Belgian colonialists without any proper preparation. The result was a predictable collapse of central government authority and chaos throughout the vast mineral-rich country.

Lumumba owed his position to elections held just before independence, but he was unable to impose his authority. The province of Katanga seceded under its leader Moise Tshombe, much of the army was mutinous, and Belgian troops remained in many parts of the Congo. Lumumba and the president, Joseph Kasavubu, appealed for outside help, and the United Nations agreed to send a force to restore order. The UN forces were not authorized to attempt to end the Katangan secession, however, so Lumumba asked the Soviet Union to give

him the tools to do the job. On 26 August about 100 Soviet-bloc technicians and 10 Il-18 Soviet transport planes arrived in the Congo.

Long before this, the United States had begun plotting Lumumba's downfall. The Congo's mineral resources were of considerable strategic importance, and Lumumba was outspoken in his anti-Americanism. The United States was increasingly concerned about the possible growth of Soviet influence in Africa. The CIA station chief in the Congo, Lawrence Devlin (codenamed Victor Hedgman), filed a report in which he expressed fears that the Congo was experiencing 'a classic communist takeover government.' At the end of this somewhat hysterical note Devlin added: 'There may be little time left in which to take action to avoid another Cuba.' The mention of Cuba was enough for the CIA. By return Devlin was cabled: 'You are authorized to proceed with operation.'

Enemies in the Congo: Moise Tshombe (above right), leader of the breakaway province of Katanga, and Patrice Lumumba (right), the country's first prime minister after independence. Lumumba adopted an anti-American stance, and getting rid of him became a CIA obsession.

Devlin sent a further cable describing how anti-Lumumba leaders had approached President Kasavubu and shown him a plan to assassinate Lumumba, but Kasavubu was not interested in this proposition. The CIA had already established standard covert actions in the Congo by this stage, including bribes to influence labor groups and an 'attempt to arrange a vote of no-confidence in Lumumba in the Congolese Senate.' The day before the arrival of the Soviet aid to Lumumba, Allen Dulles, Gordon Gray, presidential assistant for national security affairs, Livingston Merchant, under secretary of state for political affairs, John Irwin II, assistant secretary of defense, and a CIA officer, Thomas Parrott, met in Washington and agreed that 'any planning for the Congo would not necessarily rule out consideration of any particular kind of activity which might contribute to getting rid of Lumumba.' As a consequence of this meet-

ABOVE: The breakdown of order in the Congo in the early 1960s led to a nightmare of violence, with massacre and counter-massacre on all sides. Here 10 rebel soldiers, responsible for the public slaughter of two village women, are themselves beaten to death.

ing Dulles sent a cable to the Congolese capital, Leopoldville, giving Devlin 'wide authority for even more aggressive action if it can remain covert.' A sum of $100,000 was authorized as expenditure for the program.

Devlin took Dulles' advice at its face value and went ahead to cultivate anti-Lumumba factions within the Congo. On 5 September 1960 Kasavubu sacked Lumumba from government, after which army leader Colonel Joseph Mobutu came to power. The CIA approved of Mobutu and was anxious that he should remain in power, so it did not slacken in its efforts to dispose totally of Lumumba.

The UN was keen to reopen the Congolese parliament after the accession of Mobutu but the CIA feared that this parliament would probably bring Lumumba back to power. There were also worries that the Soviet Union might try forcibly to oust Mobutu and replace him with Lumumba. Consequently the Agency started to look at different ways in which Lumumba might be assassinated; the major area which they examined was the one where to date they had been least successful, that of poison. Sidney Gottlieb was approached, as he had the right qualifications, holding a PhD in bio-organic chemistry, and was also special assistant for scientific matters to the Direc-

tor of Planning, Richard Bissell. Gottlieb was consigned to develop a poison which could take on the appearances of an African disease. Having developed a suitable substance Gottlieb was dispatched to Leopoldville and instructed to provide scientific back-up for Devlin. Just in case the poison plan did not work, the Agency trained two professional hit men, known as WI/ROGUE and QJ/WIN, and prepared to send them out to the Congo as well.

Soon Gottlieb and Devlin were having all kinds of bizarre discussions as to how to get Lumumba and the poison together. Throughout these preliminary steps both Gottlieb and Devlin believed that they were acting with the express consent of the President. In a later post-mortem into the affair Devlin confirmed this supposition. As with previous planned poison plots, however, this one failed. The main problem was that they had no means to ensure that Lumumba actually took the poison. Gottlieb was also starting to worry whether or not his poisons had retained their strength, having been unrefrigerated since his arrival in Zaire. Realizing that the plan was never going to work, Gottlieb returned to the United States on 5 October.

The ever-ingenious Devlin, undeterred by the failure of the poison plot, decided that possibly a commando raid could be launch-

LEFT: Lumumba (on balcony, center left) under the protective custody of UN troops after his dismissal from government. Although Lumumba had more popular support than any other leader in the Congo, the forces pulling the country apart were too strong for him to control.

ed against Lumumba's house. He also requested that a light hunting rifle be sent out to the Congo. The man chosen by the CIA to be at the trigger end of that hunting rifle was Justin O'Donnell. He insisted that he did not wish to become any part of the CIA's plot to assassinate Lumumba, but he did agree to help try to draw Lumumba from the UN protective custody under which he had been held since Mobutu's accession in

September. Once in the Congo O'Donnell requested that QJ/WIN be sent over to assist him. Lumumba, meanwhile, had escaped from his UN custody and made his way toward his political stronghold of Stanleyville; once there Lumumba hoped to establish a base and mount a counter-coup against Mobutu.

The Mobutu government liaised with the CIA in blocking roads and alerting troops in

85

the search for Lumumba. This move proved successful, for Lumumba was captured on his way to Stanleyville and was jailed at Thysville. The activities of the CIA over Lumumba did not stop with his incarceration, however. Feelings against him were running so high in the CIA that one could say that the Agency was almost completely obsessed by the man. One plausible reason for their edginess was that there was a genuine feeling of discontent among the Congolese troops against Mobutu and it was felt by some observers that these troops might swap allegiance and back Lumumba.

Captured by his enemies, Lumumba was led around on the end of a rope (right) and eventually murdered. The ultimate beneficiary of his death was President Mobutu (conducting a bizarre press conference, below) whose corrupt and brutal regime was backed wholeheartedly by the CIA as a bastion of anti-communism.

Devlin certainly believed this was possible. It was decided to transfer Lumumba to Bakwanga, known at the time as the 'slaughterhouse' due to the many killings which had taken place there. But Lumumba never got that far. The plane in which he was travelling was redirected to Katanga where, on 17 January 1961, Lumumba was murdered.

As to who murdered him, the answer is probably his Congolese political opponents, but the finance and the backing behind these people undoubtedly stemmed from the CIA. The Church Commission, on looking into the matter, did say that 'the testimony is strong enough to permit a reasonable inference that the plot to assassinate Lumumba was authorized by President Eisenhower.' Certainly many of those involved in the project believed that authorization had come 'from the top.' As for the man that the CIA brought to power, Mobutu is now one of the world's richest men. His personal fortune is estimated to be a colossal $2,939,200,000 and his regime is constantly criticized for its atrocious human rights record. Ironically embezzlement in Zaire is punishable by the death penalty.

In southern Africa, CIA involvement has occurred in the context of the special relationship between the Agency and the South African intelligence service BOSS (Bureau of State Security). BOSS was set up in 1969 and throughout its vicious history has been closely involved with and backed by the CIA. This was admitted in 1977 by former deputy director of BOSS Alexander Van Wyk, who acknowledged that 'agents have been highly trained in the United States and West Germany; every now and then we get together and discuss our mutual interests.' The British journalist Anthony Sampson has also observed that 'the Pretoria CIA station still relies on BOSS reports about revolutionaries.'

The original BOSS brief was for that organization to investigate 'all matters affecting the security of the State' as well as become responsible for the South African security police and intelligence operations. Ultimate control lay with the prime minister,

LEFT: General Hendrik van den Bergh, head of the South African security service BOSS from its creation in 1969. Van den Bergh was an admirer of Hitler and had a reputation for extreme brutality among South African blacks.

who, in 1969, was John Vorster. General Hendrik van den Bergh was chosen to head the new service. Both Vorster and Van den Bergh had been interned by the government during World War II because of their pro-Nazi beliefs. Van den Bergh had been used by Vorster in 1963 to command the Security Police during the protest and sabotage campaigns mounted by the black liberation organizations the African National Congress (ANC) and the Pan Africanist Congress (PAC). BOSS was also assigned to take over many of the functions of both the military and police intelligence departments. Van den Bergh's reputation was fearsome; he is said to have been one of the men most hated by black South Africans, and he was actually forced to retire in 1978 when it was estimated that at least 48 black and Asian prisoners had died under his custody.

One of the main reasons for the CIA liaison with BOSS is the strategically important position occupied by South Africa. It is perfectly situated to monitor Soviet and Cuban activity in Angola and Mozambique, as well as Soviet shipping and submarine activity around the Cape of Good Hope. At one stage during this 'special relationship' BOSS was providing regular monthly reports on Soviet and Cuban activity. Representatives of the National Security Agency

(NSA) were drafted to Silvermine, a South African intelligence installation near Cape Town, and from this post the agents were able to transmit reports of Soviet activity to the NSA's US headquarters at Fort Meade; these reports were said to be relayed to the United States by GCHQ installations.

Bizarrely, Van den Bergh believed that he could torture blacks at home in South Africa but then act as a conciliator for détente with other black African states. In 1972, with the aid of Minister for Information Connie Mulder, Van den Bergh hatched a scheme whereby South Africa would either buy out or win over the opinion of African, European and US policymakers. About $73 million was paid out to Dr Eschel Rhoodie to carry out this plan. The massive campaign was run on very similar lines to those of both the CIA and the KGB when those agencies were trying to establish their propaganda machines. BOSS financed its own newspaper, *The Citizen*, to act as an English-language propaganda broadsheet. The organization also spread its activities overseas, first of all by trying to buy newspapers in the United States. To this end, $10 million was given to Michigan newspaper publisher John McGoff. McGoff initially tried to buy the *Washington Star* but had to be satisfied with the *Sacramento Union*.

In Britain BOSS infiltrated two charitable

LEFT: A South African Daphne-class submarine at the top secret Simonstown naval base. Despite an official world embargo on arms exports to South Africa, the country has developed a considerable military force, believed to include some form of nuclear capability.

BELOW: Black rioting in the South African townships has become a regular feature of life under apartheid. The main black opposition group, the ANC, is banned as a terrorist organization and is described by the white regime as a tool of international communist subversion.

organizations, Christian Aid, which works for famine relief worldwide, and the Canon Collins Trust, an educational charity which specializes in the education of black South Africans. The British government tipped off the two charities about the BOSS agents. In Norway BOSS managed to finance a small pro-South African political party. It has even been alleged that BOSS was behind the financing of the political campaigns of Gerald Ford's 1976 presidential bid, Samuel Hayakawa's 1976 US Senate race and Roger Jepsen's defeat in 1978 of Iowa senator Dick Clarke. The propaganda operation fell apart when accusations of personal gain were levelled at Mulder. After a lengthy and bitter power struggle within the ruling Nationalist Party Premier Vorster resigned, as did Mulder and Rhoodie. The Botha regime which replaced Vorster has concentrated on overcoming Western arms embargoes rather than financing massive propaganda campaigns in the Western press. This is not to say that 'planted stories' have disappeared, nor does it mean that PW Botha is any less brutal against the black majority than Vorster; he just approaches the governing of South Africa in a different but equally repressive manner. Botha also depends more on military intelligence than on BOSS, renamed the National Intelligence Service after 1978.

LEFT: Dr Eschel Rhoodie, here under arrest in France, was entrusted by BOSS with masterminding an expensive covert propaganda operation in Europe and the United States. His downfall came in 1979 with the so-called Muldergate scandal, which also led to the resignation of John Vorster.

BELOW: P W Botha, Vorster's successor as South African leader, has not substantially altered the regime, although there have been some cosmetic changes – BOSS is now the National Intelligence Service.

CIA activities in Africa as a whole have reflected a principle expressed by Richard Bissell: 'The underdeveloped world presents greater opportunities for covert intelligence collection simply because governments are much less highly orientated; there is less security consciousness; and there is apt to be more actual or potential diffusion of power among parties, localities, organizations and individuals outside the central governments.'

An area where this 'diffusion of power among parties ... and individuals outside of central government' is well illustrated is in the ravaged country of Angola. Unlike other colonial powers in Africa, Portugal refused to allow its colonies the independence which they so desperately sought. In 1961 Portugal's Prime Minister Antonio de Oliveira Salazar told the United States that 'the only nationalism in Angola and Mozambique was Portuguese,' and revolts in the Angolan capital of Luanda and in the north of the country were bloodily crushed.

The United States castigated the Portuguese for their behavior and at the UN called for a peaceful transition to power for the black nationalists. The CIA also started to supply 'financial non-military aid' to the Revolutionary Government of Angola in Exile (GRAE), headed by Holden Roberto and based in the Congolese capital, Leopoldville (now Kinshasa).

However, the policies of the US administration and the CIA soon diverged. The United States was reliant on Portugal for important military facilities on the Azores in mid-Atlantic, and after pressure from the Portuguese overt diplomatic support for Roberto ceased. By the end of the 1960s, the United States was supplying the Portuguese with aircraft for use in their counter-insurgency campaign against the black nationalists. For the CIA, however, Roberto remained a promising option. He had close links with the CIA-backed Mobutu regime in the Congo – in fact, Roberto was Mobutu's brother-in-law. The GRAE was able to use the Congo as a base for mounting a guerrilla campaign against the Portu-

The refusal of Portuguese ruler Antonio Salazar (above left) to grant independence to Angola in the early 1960s, when other European powers withdrew from their African colonies, led to a prolonged guerrilla war against nationalist movements, including UNITA (above, an eccentrically clad UNITA fighter).

guese in Angola, or rather it would have been able to, had Roberto been interested in fighting. In fact, he showed little inclination to take on the colonialists.

Recognized by the Organization of African Unity (OAU) in 1964 as the true government of Angola, GRAE's fortunes declined through the rest of the decade. In 1966 Jonas Savimbi, a former member of Roberto's movement, set up his own alter-native group, the National Union for the Total Independence of Angola (UNITA), which built up a following in the south of Angola. A third independence movement, the Popular Movement for the Liberation of Angola (MPLA), had existed since 1956 and was strongest in the center and east of the country, including the capital. During the 1960s the MPLA won the support of the Soviet Union and of many African states,

including Zambia where it had its military base. By 1969 the Portuguese saw the MPLA as by far the most serious threat to their colony, and by 1971 the OAU had withdrawn its recognition of Roberto's government-in-exile. His force still existed, however, renamed the Front for the Liberation of Angola (FNLA). Concern about the MPLA led the Portuguese to seek to make contact with the other two liberation movements, and they soon established links with UNITA which promised to 'neutralize' the Soviet-backed MPLA.

In 1974, the situation was transformed by events in Portugal itself, where a group of left-wing army officers masterminded a coup that overthrew Salazar's successor, Marcello Caetano. One of the officers' key objectives was to end Portugal's colonial wars, and it was now clearly only a matter of time

RIGHT: Secretary of State Henry Kissinger, who dominated American foreign policy under Presidents Nixon and Ford. Although keen to resist communism, Kissinger was also intent on avoiding any direct confrontation with the Soviet Union, and he counselled caution in the CIA Angolan operation.

before Angola became independent. The Portuguese forces virtually stopped fighting and the race for power between the MPLA, UNITA and FNLA began. Worried about the possibility of an MPLA victory, the administration of President Gerald Ford authorized the CIA to spend $32 million in support of the two other groups. Secretary of State Henry Kissinger insisted that absolute secrecy must be maintained, since there were legal obstacles to providing military assistance to insurgents, and overt aid could lead to 'unmanageable and overt confrontation with the Soviet Union.'

Naturally, as the CIA already had a substantial presence in Zaire (as the Congo was now called) alongside their protégé Mobutu, most of the US aid went to Roberto's FNLA. Almost half the total sum was reportedly spent on providing arms and equipment. Given the extreme corruption of Mobutu's regime, it is not surprising that much of the money never reached its des-

tination, but ended up in the pockets of Zaire's ruling elite. Support for UNITA in the south of Angola was largely left to the South Africans, with CIA encouragement.

In the run up to independence, set for 11 November 1975, a transitional coalition government was established in Luanda with the three rival groups participating, but the MPLA, strongest in the capital, quickly emerged as the dominant partner and fighting broke out, soon escalating into full-scale civil war. Roberto's CIA-equipped force, accompanied by elements of the Zairean army, invaded Angola from the north, while UNITA and South African troops advanced from the south. The MPLA was only saved by the direct intervention of a Cuban force and a massive injection of equipment from the Soviet Union.

Back in the United States Congress was becoming increasingly wary of the amount of money being pumped in to Angola, so the administration was forced to turn to Europe

LEFT: British and American mercenaries on trial in the Angolan capital, Luanda, after the disastrous failure of their intervention in the Angolan conflict. Led by the brutal 'Colonel Callan' (here gesticulating with pencil), the mercenaries briefly fought the MPLA and Cuban troops in northern Angola, but internal dissension and military inadequacies soon brought about their defeat.

BELOW: Angolan troops inspect a knocked-out Soviet APC. Soviet weapons of all types saw service in this conflict and, if nothing else, gave KGB advisors a chance to assess them in battlefield conditions.

ABOVE: The leaders of the three rival liberation movements in Angola, the Marxist Agostinho Neto (left), Holden Roberto of the FNLA (center) and the head of UNITA, Jonas Savimbi. Neto emerged as the winner in 1975, but the CIA still backed Savimbi against him, after their original favorite, Roberto, had dropped out of the running.

LEFT: A rare photo of an Eastern bloc advisor with MPLA troops. The support of the Soviet Union and Cuba was crucial to the MPLA victory and its subsequent survival against the challenge of UNITA and South Africa.

for further financial and military aid. British and other mercenaries were recruited, possibly with the approval of the British government, to try to revive Roberto's flagging military effort, and Britain was requested to send missiles – which it refused to do. Jonas Savimbi was able to get equipment from a British company, Racal Communications, however, and 'Tiny' Rowland's Lonrho company also backed UNITA, flying in military aid.

Despite the frenetic activity of the CIA and South Africa, by February 1976 the FNLA and UNITA had failed in their bid for power and the MPLA were able to establish themselves as the government of Angola. Congress totally cut off finance for the Angolan covert action and the United States and South Africa officially withdrew. In reality, however, South Africa has continued to operate on a semi-permanent basis in southern Angola in support of UNITA guerrillas, whom it arms and finances. The CIA has also continued to back Jonas Savimbi's organization in its attacks on the MPLA government, at times with, and at times without, official authorization. Holden Roberto's movement, on the other hand, has sunk without trace. Cuban troops remain in Angola in support of the MPLA regime, along with Soviet and East European advisors, although since the mid 1980s this aid has been fairly low key.

American intervention in both Angola and the Congo (Zaire) was viewed in some quarters as essential in order to combat any Soviet threat, and also imperative if the United States wanted to gain a foothold in a continent which was becoming increasingly important in world affairs. Critics have maintained that activities in these countries were carried out at too high a cost, since they jeopardized important moderate opinion in neighboring African states. Some factions in Congress also viewed CIA covert actions in Africa with growing trepidation. The Senate Select Committee on Intelligence reached the conclusion that: 'Certain covert operations have been incompatible with American principles and ideology and, when exposed, have resulted in damaging this nation's ability to exercise moral and ethical leadership.' Congress also believed that the so-called 'communist threat' was frequently overdramatized, and because of this overreaction movements which had initially been grassroots freedom movements rather than dangerous communist subversions turned to the Soviet Union for support. In the mid-1970s Zambia said of CIA activity in Africa: 'The most obscene haste with which the West has rushed to pour arms into Zaire reinforces the argument of many Africans that behind every attempted or successful coup on this continent is the hand of a foreign power.'

97

WAR IN ANGOLA

Between 1961 and 1974, three rival liberation movements, the MPLA, the FNLA and UNITA, fought a guerrilla war against the Portuguese colonial authorities in Angola. After a left-wing military coup in Portugal in April 1974, the new administration sought to hand over power, but there was no possible agreement between the Marxist MPLA and its opponents. The CIA poured money and arms into Zaire, where the FNLA was based, while South Africa backed UNITA, with the approval of the United States. The Soviet Union rushed arms to the MPLA in the Angolan capital, Luanda, and Cuban troops moved in to operate the Soviet weapons. Both the FNLA and the UNITA/South African forces were defeated by the Cubans and the MPLA in late 1975, and the MPLA established itself as the government of Angola, although the CIA and the South Africans continued to support UNITA in a guerrilla war against the new regime.

RIGHT AND BELOW RIGHT: The MPLA was armed from Soviet stocks and their equipment ranged from AK assault rifles through grenades of various types to sophisticated anti-aircraft weapons.

LEFT, BELOW LEFT AND BELOW: The rebel forces of the FNLA and UNITA relied on weapons and training from the West; both these elements varied considerably in quality.

United States activities in the Middle East also antagonized many observers. The CIA's involvement in the region has been singularly unsuccessful, marked by intelligence misjudgments and a repeated failure to influence events in the desired direction. In 1953, for example, the CIA backed the Arab nationalist Gamal Abdul Nasser when he seized power from the British-backed King Faroukh. It seemed the right move in the game whose object was to replace Britain as the dominant Western power in the region, while at the same time keeping out Soviet influence. But subsequently the situation was badly mishandled. In 1955 Nasser started to receive aid from the Soviet Union, causing both Foster Dulles and Kermit Roosevelt to fly to Cairo and try to court the Egyptian leader. Their mission failed and in response to Nasser's refusal to toe the American line, the United States pulled out of funding the vital Aswan Dam project. This infuriated

Nasser who turned to the Soviets to fund the dam and subsequently nationalized the Suez Canal, throwing the Middle East into crisis. The CIA had completely failed to predict Nasser's response to America's tough line, which had radically increased Soviet power and influence not only in Egypt, but throughout the Middle East.

The initial US support for Nasser had been opposed by the most skillful spy agency in the region, Israel's Mossad. The Arab nationalists were dedicated enemies of Israel, and in 1954 Mossad conceived a plan, known as Operation Suzanne, to ruin US-Egyptian relations. Agents were sent into Egypt to carry out attacks on American property, which could then be blamed on communists and discredit the Nasser regime. The scheme failed hopelessly and the Israeli spy network in Egypt was betrayed to its enemies. But as we have seen, events did Mossad's work for it.

The United States has subsequently

The CIA failed to understand the radical Egyptian leader Gamal Abdul Nasser (right), advocating a tough line to bring him to heel as an ally of the United States. Instead, when American finance for Nasser's Aswan Dam project was withdrawn, he nationalized the Suez Canal (above) to raise the funds and called in the Soviets to help.

Tour' round Europe, trying to confuse any-one who might be following or watching him. His final destination was Paris where he was given the brief of identifying the Egyptian factories and keeping an eye on the West Germans whom Egypt had re-cruited. In 1961, Lotz settled in Egypt and was able to penetrate the small German community in Cairo – he was himself a German by birth. He also managed to keep in constant contact with his bosses in Tel Aviv. By the end of 1962, he had been able to establish the extent of the Egyptian missile-building program and transmit many details of the project. Lotz was finally caught by the Egyptians in 1965 and imprisoned, but after the Six-Day War in 1967 he was released, along with eight other captured Israeli spies, in exchange for 5000 Egyptian prisoners of war.

Israeli Mossad agents were experts in covert operations against their Arab nationalist enemies. Wolfgang Lotz (right), known as 'the champagne spy,' provided extensive intelligence on Egyptian missile development. But it was dangerous work: in the photo above, a Mossad agent is being led out by Jordanian officials to be hanged.

become Israel's closest ally, and the CIA has maintained close contact with Mossad, which has proved itself one of the world's leaders in undercover operations. In 1960, for example, Mossad was tipped off that an Egyptian general was actively recruiting West German scientists to work on an undercover Egyptian missile project. The general was the former head of the Egyptian Air Force intelligence bureau, Mahmoud Khalil, a close friend of Nasser. Mossad learned that Khalil had succeeded in recruit-ing 26 scientists, including Dr Eugen Sänger of the Institute of Research on Jet Propul-sion in Stuttgart. A series of undercover companies was also set up by the Egyptians in order to purchase material and other essential products for the proposed missile factory. Included in this list of bogus com-panies was IntraHandel, based in Munich and Stuttgart.

Later in that year a Mossad agent, Wolf-gang Lotz, took what amounted to a 'Grand

To return to the CIA, another area where it should have trodden more carefully is Iran. By supporting the return of the Shah in 1953 the CIA was in effect backing a brutal and highly controversial regime. In 1957 the Americans helped establish Savak, the Iranian secret service, which is now commonly agreed to have formed one of the most oppressive secret police forces in the world. Political opposition to the Shah's regime was completely forbidden and protestors were tortured and murdered by Savak. The West turned a blind eye to these activities, since the Shah was such a useful ally. The CIA established a listening post to spy on the Soviet Union at Kabkan Behshar in northern Iran. It was not until President Jimmy Carter came to power in Washington in 1976 that the United States put pressure on the Shah to change his ways. Even then, the Americans completely misjudged the strength of the Muslim fundamentalists led by the exiled Ayatollah Khomeni. In January 1979 the Shah was toppled and Savak was disbanded. The CIA listening posts were deserted, left wired to blow up if any attempt was made to enter them. The fanatically anti-American Khomeni regime came to power and before the end of 1979 CIA men in the US embassy in Teheran found themselves held hostage by Iranian students. The attempt to free the hostages by force, in which the CIA was of course involved, was a fiasco. A deal was finally struck, but only after the United States had been thoroughly humiliated. The Iran crisis could have been averted had the United States understood sooner the injustices

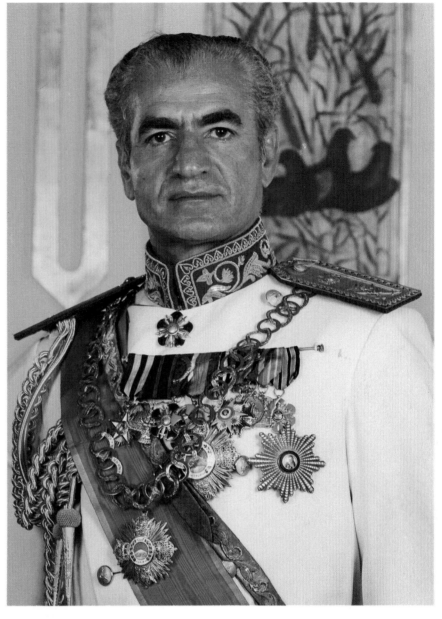

ABOVE: The Shah of Iran, Mohammed Reza Pahlavi, in full ceremonial uniform. The CIA backed the Shah to the last, sure that he would survive the unpopularity earned by his secret police, Savak, and by his pro-American policies.

LEFT: The CIA listening post in northern Iran, near the Soviet border, abandoned after the overthrow of the Shah in January 1979.

RIGHT: Ayatollah Khomeni is greeted by a crowd of supporters on his return to Iran after years of exile in Paris. The CIA failed to accurately assess his importance as a force for change in Iran.

BELOW: Iranian students occupying the US Embassy in Iran rejoice at the burning of the American National flag. For these theological radicals, America represented all that was evil in the world.

LEFT: Enterprising young Iranians engage in selling anti-American propaganda outside the captured US Embassy.

BELOW: The Iranian Revolution led to widespread street fighting, such as this gun battle in the city of Khorramshar.

being perpetrated by the Shah and given its support to the democratic opposition. Instead, the United States lost yet another vital ally within the troubled Middle East arena.

In terms of strategy, the CIA's bullish approach in both the Middle East and Africa has played right into the hands of the KGB. Countries which might have remained neutral or friendly were flung into the arms of the KGB by the CIA's dogmatic approach to international affairs. The CIA has been shown to have been totally misguided in its 'red phobia'; by replacing left-wing regimes with dictatorial right-wing leaders, the CIA has frequently done the United States' image more harm than good and has increased the possibility of Soviet penetration rather than reduced it.

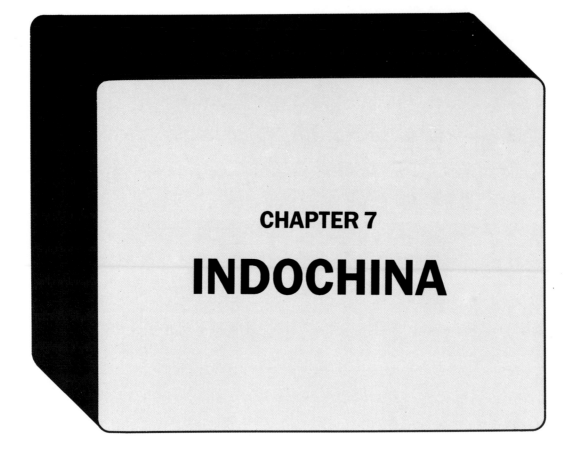

CHAPTER 7

INDOCHINA

RIGHT: The father of modern Vietnam, Ho Chi Minh, photographed during the war against the French colonial power that ended in 1954. Even his enemies admitted that Ho was the most popular political figure in Vietnam.

FAR RIGHT: A Vietnamese guerrilla poses for the camera. These lightly armed soldiers showed extraordinary courage and endurance in the war against the technologically advanced US forces.

It was with growing unease that the United States watched the rise and spread of communism in east Asia in the postwar years, with Mao Tse-tung's victory in China in 1949 and the North Korean invasion of South Korea the following year. In 1953, the CIA tried to organize resistance inside China against the communist government, but two agents, John Downey and Richard Fecteau, were arrested by the Chinese authorities and the operation was a failure.

Partly as a result of this setback, the Agency then turned its attention to French Indochina – Vietnam, Laos and Cambodia. The French colonial administration was on the point of losing a long-drawn-out guerrilla war mounted by the communist-led Viet Minh. The communist leader, Ho Chi Minh, had achieved massive popularity among the Vietnamese people. President Eisenhower even wrote: 'I have never talked or corresponded with a person knowledgeable in Indochinese affairs who did not

ABOVE: French paratroopers jump into Dien Bien Phu, deep in northern Vietnam. Surrounded by Viet Minh forces, the French were worn down and finally completely overrun in May 1954. The defeat at Dien Bien Phu sealed the collapse of French power in Indochina.

agree that had elections been held as of the time of the fighting, possibly 80 percent of the population would have voted for Ho Chi Minh.' The Americans were determined to prevent a communist victory, however, and prepared to take over responsibility for resistance to Ho Chi Minh after the inevitable French collapse. Eisenhower and Secretary of State Dulles chose Colonel Edward Lansdale, a former OSS man, to select a leader for the Vietnamese and to guarantee that leader whatever US support would be needed to keep him in power. Lansdale concluded that the current prime minister, Ngo Dinh Diem, had sufficient qualities to fulfill US wishes. In May 1954 the French were totally routed at the battle of Dien Bien Phu and Indochina became independent. Vietnam was, supposedly temporarily, divided into two halves, the North ruled by Ho Chi Minh and the South by Emperor Bao Dai and Prime Minister Diem. Immediately after independence, the CIA

mounted a classic 'dirty tricks' campaign in the North to spread panic among the minority Catholic part of the population. Scare stories were published, false horoscopes circulated and rumors started, to such effect that some 800,000 people emigrated to the South.

At the same time, in the South Lansdale helped Diem build up his personal power. By October 1955 Diem had routed his opponents and was able to have himself elected president in place of the discredited Emperor Dai. Not all Americans involved in the Vietnam situation approved of the policy of support for Diem as sole ruler. Former Chief of Staff General Lawton Collins, for example, favored the establishment of a coalition government. But once Diem was in control, there was no one who could feasibly replace him. He set up a corrupt and repressive regime, backed with US aid totalling over $1 billion in 1955-60. Diem's brother Ngo Dinh Nhu was also

established as a leading political force and it was through him that the CIA exercised its influence within Vietnam.

Despite US backing, Diem's regime became increasingly insecure. By 1959 an extensive guerrilla campaign threatened control of the countryside, and opposition from the majority Buddhist population to Diem's Catholic regime grew in the early 1960s. The CIA chief in Saigon, William Colby, organized the Strategic Hamlets Program, a system of fortified villages throughout South Vietnam designed to protect the rural population from communist influence, but under Nhu's direction the strategic hamlets quickly degenerated into little more than concentration camps. The CIA was also involved in training and arming tribesmen in the remote mountain regions of western Vietnam, the Montagnards, to form an anti-communist defense force. But South Vietnam was too rotten to be shored up by such measures for long.

Thai irregulars joined the French at Dien Bien Phu (above), emphasizing the significance of the battle for the whole of southeast Asia. After the French withdrawal, the United States moved in to prevent the area going communist, and Colonel Edward Lansdale (left) organized support for the government of Ngo Dinh Diem in South Vietnam.

The US Administration started to doubt the wisdom of having supported the Diem dynasty, and the mounting conflict with the Buddhists brought matters to a head. In 1963 Diem's home was the focus of demonstrations by Buddhists angry at having their rights constantly violated by Diem's regime. Nhu's Special Forces opened fire on the demonstrators and also attacked Buddhist pagodas and temples; Buddhist monks burned themselves to death on the streets. This was an embarrassing situation for the United States, given that most Vietnamese realized that the CIA was responsible for arming and supporting the Special Forces.

In November 1963 the Diem brothers were deposed and assassinated; conjecture was rife as to whether or not the CIA had been directly involved in the coup. In 1971, when the Pentagon Papers were leaked to the press, it was clearly revealed that the CIA had played a major part in the destabilization of the Diem regime. In one of the documents CIA headquarters orders the US ambassador to Vietnam, Henry Cabot Lodge, to 'preserve deniability in all contacts with plotters'. The documents also revealed that the CIA had worked very closely with the Vietnamese generals who had carried out the coup. After the Diem debacle the United States and the CIA continued to pump more arms and men into Vietnam until, by 1965, the situation had escalated from the political propping up of a weak anti-communist regime to a full-scale devastating war.

BELOW: President Diem (seated) accepts the homage of his subjects in a 1956 ceremony. Diem's Catholicism was alien to the beliefs of most of the South Vietnamese population.

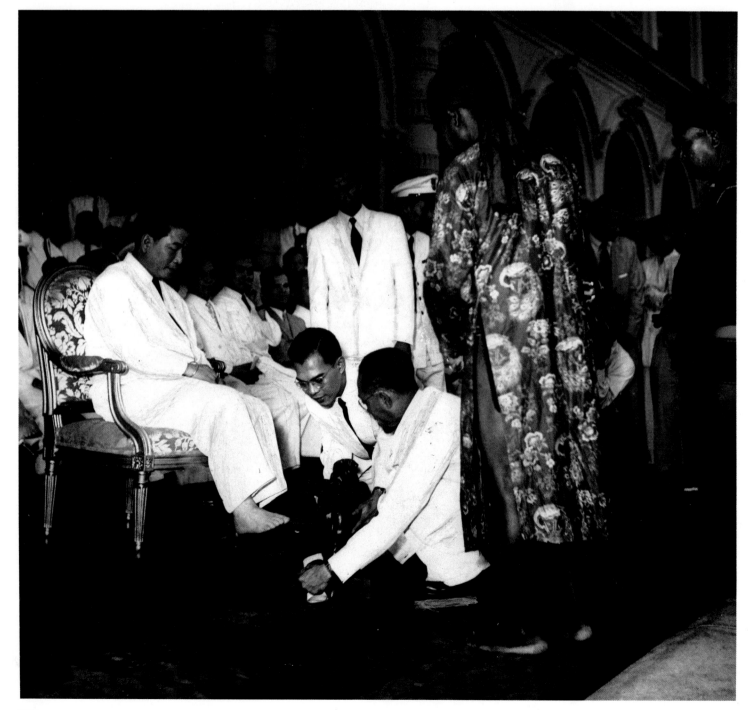

LEFT: A contingent of South Vietnamese troops, flown into a Viet Cong area by US pilots, sets fire to a building recently vacated by the guerrillas. The South Vietnamese Army proved totally ineffectual in these early combats.

BELOW: A Buddhist monk burns himself to death in protest at the anti-Buddhist policies of the Diem regime in 1963. Such pictures had a profound impact on world opinion and convinced many US policymakers that it was impossible to go on backing Diem.

Meanwhile, the CIA had also become actively entangled in another part of Indochina, Laos. After the French withdrawal in 1954, control of the country had passed into the hands of a neutralist government under Prince Souvanna Phouma. But by 1958 the communist Pathet Lao had made significant electoral gains and the CIA had decided to back right-wing elements against Souvanna, whose policy was to include the communists in government. In 1958 right-wing generals duly took power and the Pathet Lao went into armed opposition. The CIA's favorite general was Phoumi Nosavan, and he was in control in August 1960 when a force of 300 men led by a 26-year-old army captain named Kong Lae carried out a dramatic coup. Lae invited

BELOW: A Meo tribesman armed by the CIA. The use of the various mountain tribes of Indochina to combat communist guerrillas was a great success in the short term, but it exposed the tribesmen to awful retribution as American power in the region waned.

Souvanna to return to power, but Phoumi still clung to territory in the south of Laos and could boast the support of the Royal Lao Forces. Additional help for Phoumi came from his personal CIA aide Jack Hazey.

Up in the north of the country Kong Lae was active in persuading Souvanna Phouma to form a coalition government; General Phoumi and his vice-president were also invited to join. The US ambassador, Winthrop Brown, urged the United States to support the new government but the CIA decided to continue in its support of Phoumi. This precipitated Phoumi to refuse to negotiate with Souvanna and also left Souvanna without an army. The government was short of food and medical supplies as well as military equipment. To make matters worse, the United States demanded that Souvanna abandon his neutralist stand and oppose the Pathet Lao. Souvanna refused to comply with these instructions. After protracted pleading with the United States for aid, Souvanna was forced to appeal to the Soviet Union. The Soviets were delighted with this request as it would give them a foothold in southern Asia and provide them with an opportunity to usurp Chinese influence in the area. A Soviet airlift from Hanoi was organized in 1961 – the Russians had arrived.

This action by the Soviets produced an immediate reaction from the US-backed Phoumi who rapidly marched northward to recapture the Laotian capital of Vientiane. Both Souvanna and Kong Lae retreated from the capital. Surprisingly Phoumi did not chase the retreating Lae, so in 1961 Kong Lae was still free and available to join up with the Soviet-armed forces of the Pathet Lao. The combined forces were joined by North Vietnamese guerrillas who enabled them to capture an airstrip on the Plain of Jars. This airstrip was of vital importance to Hanoi since it was only 50 miles away from the North Vietnamese border.

Back in the United States a new President had come to power: John F Kennedy was inaugurated on 19 January 1961. One of the new President's first acts was to ask his aides to draw up a plan to 'save Laos.' The aides devised a plan whereby Allied forces would take over the defense of Vientiane under the authority of the Southeast Asia Treaty Organization. This policy, though, was undermined by the President himself who unilaterally ordered the Seventh Fleet to station itself within striking distance of Laos. This action was not guaranteed to urge the Allied forces to support the United States, and indeed Britain and France decided that they did not want to give military

support to the President. Kennedy counter-attacked by going on national TV on March 23 and stating that Western powers would 'have to consider their response if the communist attack continued in Laos.'

Partly as a result of this broadcast and partly from a fear of direct confrontation with the United States, the Soviet Union agreed to a ceasefire as arranged by the British. In May 1961 a 14-nation conference was convened in Geneva to discuss Laos. At this conference it was agreed to work for a neutral and independent Laos; Souvanna Phouma was to be recalled and asked to form a government which would involve all the Laotian factions including both the communist Pathet Lao and the forces commanded by General Phoumi. But Phoumi refused to have any part in this government, believing instead that the United States and, more specifically, the CIA would support him in an independent bid for power. Perturbed by this response the new director of the CIA, John A McCone, ordered his men out of Laos. Undeterred General Phoumi embarked on a disastrous mission within Pathet Lao territory. Ambassador

LEFT: A soldier of the Laotian Royal Army undergoes training by US advisors. Official American policy in Laos was often at odds with the more active line pursued independently by the CIA.

BELOW: President Kennedy delivers a televised briefing on the situation in Laos, issuing a veiled threat of military intervention to face the communist insurgency. At the time, in 1961, it was Laos, not Vietnam, that was the focus of American concern in Indochina.

RIGHT: A CIA helicopter flies into Long Cheng, the base of General Vang Pao's army of Meo tribesmen in Laos. The CIA's operation in Laos was one of the largest it had ever undertaken, creating and then supplying a force 30,000-strong. Long Cheng was turned into the second largest city in the country, out of virtually nothing.

Brown warned him that this action was highly provocative and also that the Pathet Lao would be able to annihilate his forces with the greatest of ease. Brown was proved correct and the communists successfully routed Phouma's forces.

This action eventually convinced Phoumi that he could not go it alone and it also contributed to Kennedy's decision to order 5000 US troops to take up positions on the Thai/Laos border. Finally on 11 June the three sides in the Laos conflict agreed to form a government and the decision was ratified by the Geneva Accords, which were signed on 23 July. That October the United States agreed to withdraw the 666 military

advisors attached to Phoumi's army. In March 1963, however, the Geneva Accords broke down when North Vietnam refused to withdraw troops which it had supplied to support the Pathet Lao. A new offensive commenced and the Plain of Jars was brought under communist control.

As a result of the breakdown of the accord a vicious series of war games started and the CIA rebuilt its control in Laos. At a cost of $70 million the CIA embarked on a massive program of support for local Meo tribesmen under General Vang Pao to resist the Pathet Lao. In 1963 the Meo forces expanded from a few small guerrilla bands to a huge force of 30,000 men with battalion-size units and operations. The Meo were supplied with transport and arms through the CIA's proprietary airline, Air America. The Laos operations were largely conducted through a subsidiary, Civil Air Transport (CAT). At its zenith CAT employed 5000 personnel and controlled 165 aircraft. As well as playing a major part in CIA covert actions in Laos and other parts of southeast Asia, Air America was also reputed to be involved with illegal narcotics trading operations, although some of the airline's activities were straightforward, such as the running and administration of the maintenance base at Udorn, in Thailand, which would eventually assist in the US evacuation of Saigon.

Another Air America company was Air Asia Co, based in Taiwan. Air Asia ran the largest aircraft maintenance and repair facility in southeast Asia, employing at its peak 6000 workers. Air Asia not only serviced aircraft for Air America but also for the US military. Pacific Engineering Co was also a part of Air America, providing supervising engineers for local work teams assigned to build airstrips for Vietnam as well as the covert war in Laos.

With this massive logistic back-up, the CIA was able to use the Meo in a full-scale war against the Pathet Lao and North Vietnamese troops in Laos. The Meos also defended vital US Air Force navigational beacons on Laotian mountaintops that helped in the bombing campaign against the Ho Chi Minh Trail. The great losers in this conflict were eventually the Meo themselves. By 1971 the tide of the war had turned and the CIA-backed tribesmen suffered a series of defeats. Finally, in 1973, they were totally abandoned in the general US withdrawal from Indochina. By the mid-1970s, the Meo population in Laos was reckoned to have fallen from an original quarter of a million to about 10,000.

By 1975 the major companies involved in Air America had been sold off, some of them even being sold as private airlines to ex-CIA men for their own personal use. In the early 1960s Walter Lippmann of the *Washington Post* writing about the activities of the CIA in Laos had said: 'I venture to argue that the reason we are on the defensive in so many places is that for some ten years we have used money and arms in a long, losing attempt to stabilize native governments which, in the name of anti-communism, are opposed to all social change. This has been exactly what Mr Khruschev's dogma calls for – that communism should be the only alternative to the status quo with its immemorial poverty and privilege.' In fact many commentators agreed that the CIA had too often played into the hands of the enemy they were so assiduously fighting, and in the process giving the communists what they wanted on a plate, often in places where they would not have envisaged that they could have met with any possible success.

BELOW: Young communist guerrillas of the Pathet Lao advance through mountainous terrain. The CIA's Meo army was able to stop the Pathet Lao taking power in Laos and protect US navigational facilities directing bombing missions in the area, but the communists succeeded in defending the Ho Chi Minh Trail, North Vietnam's supply route through eastern Laos, from land attack.

ABOVE: Prince Norodom Sihanouk, leader of Cambodia, whose efforts to stay neutral during the Vietnam War met with disapproval from the United States. Sihanouk was a man of many parts, noted for his saxophone playing and for his ambitions as a filmmaker – he used thousands of his people as extras in an epic.

Cambodia, the other of the trio of Indochinese states, is a case in point. As the Vietnam War grew in intensity, the United States became dissatisfied with the attitude of Cambodia's leader Prince Norodom Sihanouk, who tried to maintain a policy of neutrality although the North Vietnamese were using his territory as a safe refuge and a supply route into South Vietnam. CIA involvement in Cambodia was a response to this situation. In 1965 the *New York Times* commented that US activities in Vietnam and in neighboring countries were causing great concern among leaders of those countries: 'There is an array of southeast Asia leaders, once good friends of the United States, who are now bitter critics.' Among these leaders the paper mentioned Prince Sihanouk of Cambodia. The paper went on to add: 'There is a remarkable similarity in the complaints that were lodged by these leaders as they drifted away from the United States. For example they have all charged that the CIA conducted hostile operations against their governments during periods of ostensibly correct relations with the United States.'

Sihanouk had good reason to be concerned, for later in 1965 the CIA successfully organized a propaganda campaign to overthrow the Sukarno government in neighboring Indonesia while at the same time offering military aid to anti-Sukarno rebels. Sukarno was later deposed and the new CIA-sponsored government organized a massacre of over 500,000 members of the Indonesian Communist Party to ensure that there could be no opposition to the new Suharto regime. Unknown to Sihanouk the CIA had also been arming Cambodian rebels, the Khmer Serai, with transmitters in order to mount a campaign against him.

After the overthrow of Sihanouk by Lon Nol (left) in March 1970, the security situation in Cambodia rapidly deteriorated, and the notorious Pol Pot (right) was able to take power at the head of the communist Khmer Rouge in April 1975.

BELOW: Young Khmer Rouge line up in the Cambodian capital, Phnom Penh, after the communist victory in 1975. It is believed that millions of Cambodians died of malnutrition, ill-treatment or deliberate extermination under the Pol Pot regime.

RIGHT: Pathet Lao guerrillas in a relaxed mood. Laos fell to the communists, along with Cambodia and South Vietnam, in 1975 and all the CIA's efforts came to nothing.

Members of the Khmer Serai were later hired by the CIA for various covert missions against the government.

In March 1970 the government of Prince Sihanouk was at last overthrown by a group of anti-communist officers led by Premier Lon Nol. Lon Nol had allegedly been approached by the United States and asked if he would overthrow the neutral Sihanouk regime. Sihanouk has always maintained that this action was supported and funded by the CIA and in 1973 made public his claims in his book *My War with the CIA*. According to US Navy intelligence specialist Samuel Thornton, the CIA set up a covert operation called (somewhat unoriginally) Dirty Tricks which had the long-term role of recruiting rebel Khmer Kampuchean Krom mercenaries and instructing them to infil-trate the Cambodian Army and provide military support for the coup. Thornton maintains that Lon Nol was also asked to assist in a Sihanouk assassination plan but was unwilling for such a plan to be put into action. Sihanouk was out of the country at the time of the coup and thus managed to avoid being murdered. The coup led to an upsurge of warfare in Cambodia. Eventually the disintegration of the country brought a defeat for Lon Nol in 1975 which ushered in the horrendous dictatorship of the now notorious Pol Pot regime. In 1977, former Secretary of State Henry Kissinger effec-tively admitted US involvement in the dis-astrous overthrow of Sihanouk's govern-ment when he said: 'The United States was not involved in Sihanouk's overthrow, at least not at top level.'

BELOW: A grim meeting of the National Security Council as the communists overrun South Vietnam in April 1975. Those present include William Colby (far left), by then director of the CIA, but previously the Agency's head of operations in Vietnam. Despite repeated American assurances of continuing support for South Vietnam, they did nothing to prevent the country's collapse.

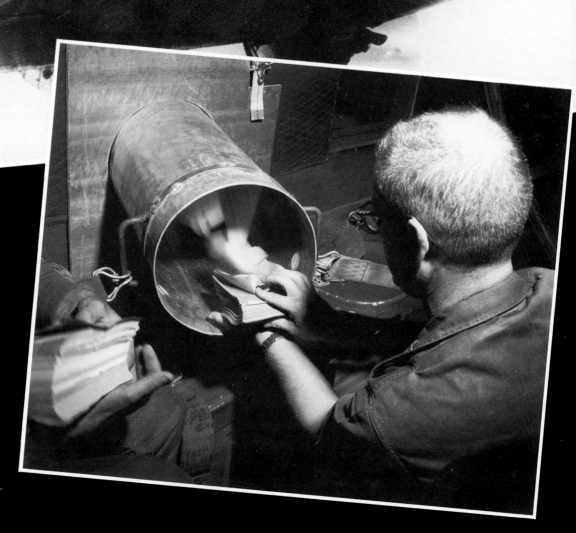

In the early days of
America's war in Vietnam,
great faith was put in the
effectiveness of
propaganda to sway the
population in favor of the
US-backed Saigon
government. The CIA
masterminded the mass
distribution of leaflets by
air. They were released
from the rear of C-47
transports (above), after
being fed into the aircraft's
dispersal chute by hand
(right).

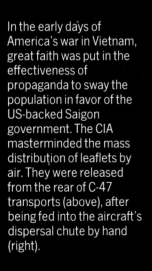

THE SECRET AIR WAR

Throughout American involvement in the war in Indochina, the covert operations conducted by the CIA were facilitated by the use of aircraft on a large scale. This progressed from the aerial distribution of propaganda leaflets in the early 1960s, when the CIA was much concerned with winning 'hearts and minds' in Vietnam, to the massive effort to inhibit supplies passing down the Ho Chi Minh Trail from North to South Vietnam through Laos. The CIA's own airline, Air America, carried out a large-scale operation to supply Meo tribesmen in Laos, armed and organized by the CIA to carry out attacks toward the Trail and protect forward navigation beacons. Yet despite all the technological marvels developed and deployed by the United States, the North Vietnamese ran into few serious difficulties with logistics.

Much ingenuity went into attempts to block the North Vietnamese supply route, the Ho Chi Minh Trail (below). Very sophisticated sensors (left and far left) were distributed along the Trail. When they registered the movement of men and material, an air strike could be called in.

But the most important field of conflict in Indochina was always Vietnam itself. The CIA organized a whole variety of operations during the critical years of the war, starting with covert raids into North Vietnam and along the North Vietnamese coast in the 1961-64 period that played a major part in the escalation of the conflict. All efforts to organize networks inside North Vietnam eventually ended in failure, however, as did extraordinary plans for coups against the Hanoi leadership, ranging from a plot to poison the Hanoi police chief with a doc-tored bottle of apricot brandy to a plan for the abduction of the entire North Vietna-mese government. The introduction of the US Army into Vietnam in 1965 inevitably overshadowed the importance of CIA operations, although there were over 1000 operatives in Saigon at the height of the war. CIA experts were constantly at odds with the military over the correct means of fighting the war. The CIA was pessimistic, and therefore accurate, in its assessment of the probable impact of large-scale US mili-tary operations, and struggled to construct

BELOW: A member of the US Special Forces training hill tribesmen in Vietnam. The hostility between the hill people and the ethnic Vietnamese of all political colors made them ready to co-operate with the Americans, but not with the Saigon government after the US troops pulled out.

CIA activities in Vietnam ranged from sophisticated intelligence gathering in remote areas of the country (above, a base camp in the mountains) to the organization and analysis of the interrogation of guerrillas and suspected communists (left). Operation Phoenix, a concerted program to identify and track down Viet Cong elements in government-held towns and villages, led to the deaths of 25,000 Vietnamese.

The hurried evacuation of American personnel from Saigon as the North Vietnamese Army advanced on the city was a public humiliation for the United States. As helicopters lifted evacuees from the roof of the US embassy (main picture), panicking Vietnamese civilians struggled to break into the embassy compound (inset left).

an alternative strategy based on intelligence and counter-insurgency techniques.

From 1968 William Colby, as CIA station-chief in Saigon, ran the Phoenix program, an attempt at 'accelerated pacification' by identifying and arresting or otherwise eliminating communists in the villages of South Vietnam. According to Colby, Phoenix was essentially an intelligence operation: all sources of information were to be centralized and analyzed so that communist cadres could be identified accurately. In Colby's view, this was both more effective and more humane than the military method of just bombing a village flat. But others, including Frank Snepp, a senior CIA agent in Saigon at the time, felt that Phoenix was little more than an excuse for a reign of terror by South Vietnamese Provincial Reconnaissance Units (PRUs), hit teams directed by the CIA. According to Snepp, CIA agents were frequently present during the torture of suspected communists, and the PRUs often shot suspects out of hand, until Phoenix became in effect a campaign of assassination. In all some 25,000 people were killed under Phoenix.

When the US Army left Vietnam in 1973, the CIA remained. Its operatives in Saigon were among the last people ferried out from the US embassy roof as the victorious North Vietnamese entered the city on 30 April 1975. In the final panic, the files containing the names of CIA informants were not destroyed, a last betrayal that seems a fitting conclusion to the US relationship with Indochina over the previous two decades. The Indochina debacle was to be a major factor in provoking a reassessment of the CIA in the United States and restrictions on its activities in the late 1970s. Interference in other countries' internal affairs would, however, soon be back in fashion.

CHAPTER 8

BACKYARD POLICIES

RIGHT: General Ivan Aleksander Serov, KGB chief in 1956 when the Soviet Union brutally crushed the uprising in Hungary. Serov's main associate in organizing the arrest of the Hungarian leadership was the then Soviet ambassador to Hungary, Yuri Andropov.

Both of the superpowers have consistently regarded the countries neighboring them, or the countries which come under their direct sphere of influence, as their own 'backyards.' They often act as if this geographical or political proximity gives them a supreme right to interfere in those countries' affairs. In the case of the Soviet Union, the so-called 'satellite states' of Poland, Czechoslovakia, East Germany, Hungary, Romania and Bulgaria, all come under the Soviet sphere of influence; if one of them steps out of line in terms of political thought and tries to water down the Soviet influence on its domestic affairs, it encounters extreme Soviet pressure to 'return to the fold.' In a similar fashion the United States has tried to dominate the affairs of all the countries of Latin America.

In 1956 the Soviet Union carried out a brutal act of repression against the state of Hungary which shocked the whole world. It was engineered by the head of the newly

LEFT: Hungarian Prime Minister Imre Nagy addresses parliament. Although Nagy was a communist he sided with the rebellion against Soviet domination and was later executed after the uprising had been suppressed.

BELOW: Soviet tanks roll through the streets of the Hungarian capital, Budapest, in November 1956. There was some heavy fighting before the tanks finally got the upper hand.

ABOVE: Hungarians express their feelings by burning Soviet flags, Budapest, 1956. The Soviet Union considered control over Eastern Europe essential to its defenses and would offer no concessions to the local population. The Soviet-installed national governments bore the brunt of popular criticism for executing their masters' orders.

reorganized KGB, General Ivan Aleksander Serov. Serov was born of a peasant family but received an education at the Frunze Academy after joining the Red Army. In 1939 he was transferred to the secret police and was in charge of the 'Sovietization' of the captured Baltic Republics. He later transferred to the Ukraine where he met and worked with the local leader, Nikita Khrushchev; it was through this earlier association that Serov gained his promotion to head of the KGB.

The Hungarian uprising was essentially an attempt by the Hungarian people to take control of the country's affairs rather than have to adhere to Moscow's wishes and demands. For the short period while it lasted the Hungarian rebels succeeded in breaking down the imposed party apparatus, dismantling the secret police and replacing party leaders with non-party men. Prime Minister Imre Nagy broke with Moscow and sided with the people. All of this was deeply disturbing to the Soviets, who feared that if Hungary were seen to be successful in its bid to throw off the yoke other East European countries would try to follow suit.

The West declared its support for the Hungarian rebels, and both the CIA and the West German BND promised to supply them with arms. The CIA was also responsible for encouraging the hopes and aspira-

tion of emigré Hungarians, promising them that the revolt had a good chance of success. The CIA-backed Radio Free Europe broadcast anti-Soviet propaganda and promised American aid to the rebels. This threat of US intervention was too much for the Soviet Union and, in November 1956, precipitated the arrival of Soviet tanks on the streets of the Hungarian capital, Budapest. Soon tales of torture and brutality started to seep out to the West, and Austria was besieged with fleeing rebels seeking asylum from the Soviet invasion. The KGB was instrumental in the removal of Nagy from power. Serov arranged a dinner for Hungarian and Soviet representatives in Budapest, ostensibly to discuss how best to negotiate the removal of Soviet tanks from the streets. Half way through dinner Serov and his men burst in on the unsuspecting diners and arrested both Prime Minister Nagy and the new Hungarian defense chief, General Pal Maleter. The Soviet negotiator General Mikhail Malinin protested, possibly because he had not known of the KGB plot, but to no avail. Maleter was later tried and then executed along with hundreds of other Hungarian dissidents. As a result of the Soviet invasion, repression in Hungary was stepped up and any thoughts neighboring satellites might have had about decreasing Soviet influence in their countries were abruptly killed.

The Soviet Union's next full-scale military intervention in its East European 'backyard' came in 1968. The Stalinist President of Czechoslovakia, Antonín Novotný, was forced to relinquish power early in the year by a liberal element inside the Czechoslovakian communist movement led by Alexander Dubček. The new regime of Dubček wanted to stay within the framework of communist party rule and the Warsaw Pact alliance with the Soviet Union, but sought to liberalize cultural life and carry out economic reforms. The communist leadership wanted to serve the needs of Czechoslovakia, instead of having forcibly to adapt themselves at all times to the wishes of Moscow. The idea of 'socialism with a human face' did not go down well with the Soviet leadership, however, and the KGB-dominated Czech secret police obviously had most to fear from the upsurge of criticism directed at 'police despotism' as censorship was abandoned.

The KGB, as the source of political intelligence, must have been involved in the eventual Soviet decision to invade Czechoslovakia on 20 August 1968. Certainly, KGB chief Yuri Andropov was one of the first

ABOVE: Czech communist leader Alexander Dubček (right) with the country's president, Ludvik Svoboda. Although proclaiming his eternal loyalty to the Soviet Union and the Warsaw Pact, Dubček tried to introduce major reforms of the communist system in Czechoslovakia during 1968. It was too much for the Soviet government to accept.

LEFT: Twelve years after the invasion of Hungary, Soviet tanks were once more on the streets of an East European city, this time Prague, the capital of Czechoslovakia. The arrival of the Soviet Army brought an abrupt end to the 'Prague Spring' of 1968.

ABOVE: Soviet troops in Prague met only passive resistance from the population, since an armed uprising seemed futile. In 1956 the CIA's Radio Free Europe had encouraged the Hungarians to fight by false promises of American help; this mistake was not repeated in the case of Czechoslovakia in 1968.

senior Soviet officials to enter Prague after the Soviet tanks, and the KGB was soon directing its local colleagues in a systematic purge of those who might oppose the Soviet presence. The heavy-handedness of the KGB prompted many defections, including the high-ranking spy Ladislav Bittman, deputy director of disinformation. The saddest image of the failure of the 'Prague Spring' is of the young student, Jan Palach, who burnt himself to death on Wenceslaus Square. For many Czechs this symbol of sacrifice reflected the gloom into which the country had been plunged after the Warsaw Pact takeover.

The CIA was criticized for not having anticipated the Czech invasion. The 1976 Pike report on the CIA found that the Agency had actually 'lost the Russian Army for two weeks' prior to the invasion, despite all the expensive gadgetry which it had at its command, as well as the Eastern spy network. The first that President Johnson

learned of the invasion was when Soviet ambassador Dobrynin visited the White House and told him. Pike surmised that 'the agencies were not up to the critical task of divining Soviet intentions.' In response Director Helms stated that he was 'not happy about those two weeks' when he could not locate Soviet troops. Helms added that 'the record would have been better if West Germany had been the target rather than Czechoslovakia.' This seems small comfort.

Possibly one reason for the CIA's failure to detect the build-up to the Soviet invasion of Czechoslovakia was that the Agency was too busy in other spheres of the world, especially in Indochina and in the United States' own backyard, Latin America. As the events in Guatemala in 1954 had shown, the United States was well prepared to intervene in Central and South America against any threat to its own interests or any suggestion of the spread of communism.

LEFT: A member of the Uruguayan Tupamaros urban guerrilla movement under arrest. The CIA helped train the Uruguayan police and counter-insurgency forces, and acted as advisors during the brutal campaign to eradicate the Tupamaros.

BELOW: In 1965 the United States sent troops to the Dominican Republic in the Caribbean, to determine the outcome of a political crisis. A force from Latin America, including Brazilians shown here, took over from the Americans once the situation was stabilized.

After Castro's rise to power in Cuba in 1959, however, US concern about the region took on a new intensity. Under President Kennedy, a dual policy was initiated with on the one hand intensive training for Latin American counter-insurgency and police forces, and on the other an attempt at support for democratization and social progress. But the two proved incompatible, as the forces trained by the CIA, the FBI and the US military crushed democracy wherever it raised its head and blocked all social reform, so that they could put into practice the techniques, including torture, that they had been taught. The CIA was involved either directly or through those it had instructed in such events as the imposition of military government on Brazil in 1964, the defeat of Che Guevara's guerrillas in Bolivia in 1967, and the campaign against the Tupamaros urban guerrillas in Uruguay from 1968 to 1973, which ended in the replacement of democratic government by yet another US-backed military regime. But the classic case of CIA intervention in Latin America was undoubtedly Chile.

Chile had a long tradition of democratic government, and when Kennedy was scouting around for a Latin American country suitable for US backing in the early 1960s, he decided on Chile as the most laudable contrast to Cuba. But even in Chile, the Americans were worried. The 1964 presidential elections were to be contested by a Marxist doctor of considerable political experience, Salvador Allende, at the head of a coalition of left-wing parties. It seemed imperative to the US government that Allende should lose. Against him stood

RIGHT: Salvador Allende in the 1960s, later to be president of Chile. An experienced politician and convinced democrat, Allende confronted the United States with the embarrassing prospect of a popularly elected communist ruler.

BELOW: President Richard Nixon and Secretary of State Kissinger. Nixon was appalled when Allende won the 1970 presidential election in Chile, and instructed CIA chief Richard Helms to subvert the Chilean government if possible.

Eduardo Frei, a reforming Christian Democrat – in Latin American terms, something of a liberal. The CIA was set to work to ensure that Frei won the election. As well as providing almost half the funds for Frei's election campaign (Frei himself was apparently unaware of these contributions), the Agency ran a powerful propaganda campaign against Allende, depicting him as a Stalinist would-be despot and a tool of Moscow. Frei was elected.

However, there were powerful American interests that were still not satisfied. Several

of the big US corporations were involved in Chile, including ITT (International Telephone and Telegraph, which was headed by John McCone when he left his post as director of the CIA), and Pepsi Cola, run by Richard Nixon's friend Donald Kendall. Kennedy had offered companies like these assurances that if they invested in Chile they would never be expropriated by the Chilean government,but the companies remained concerned that Frei, as a genuine democrat, might push through policies like profit-sharing for workers.

So US business interests decided they did not wish Frei to run in the 1970 elections, in which Allende would again be a candidate. When Nixon became US President in January 1969, the Business Group for Latin America urged him to adopt a far-right candidate, Jorge Alessandri, in preference to Frei. The business conglomerate agreed to put up $500,000 toward the 1970 elections but the State Department did not wish to accept this money. Thwarted, the combine turned its attentions toward the CIA and through the Agency they were able to donate $700,000 to the Alessandri camp. Of the donors, ITT alone gave $350,000. These actions outraged the US ambassador in Chile, Edward Korry, who mistrusted Allende's policies, but had an innate sense of democracy and fair play and believed that the Chilean people would be best left to carry out their own elections without US interference. Korry constantly found himself at odds with the CIA chief of station in Chile, Henry Heckscher, who wanted the United States to give direct support to Alessandri. Despite his misgivings, however, Korry was eventually so alarmed by the prospect of Allende ruling Chile that he went along with Heckscher's plans.

The Business Group also stepped up its activities on behalf of Alessandri and by July 1970 ITT had offered the CIA $1 million to support him; the National Security Council voted a further $500,000 for the CIA in Chile. Despite this massive pro-Alessandri campaign, however, Allende won the September elections gaining 36.3 percent to Alessandri's 34.9 percent, a third candidate with pro-Allende leanings gaining 27.8 percent of the vote. The result was enough to drive the United States and ITT into a state of frenzied panic, and subsequently CIA director Helms received the following instructions from Nixon:

One in 10 chance perhaps, but save Chile!
Worth spending
Not concerned risks involved

No involvement of embassy
$10,000,000 available, more if necessary
Full-time job – best men we have
Game plan
Make the economy scream
48 hours for plan of action.

Helms later said of these instructions: 'If I ever carried a marshal's baton in my knapsack out of the Oval Office it was that day.'

The plan of action which the CIA came up with was a military coup, to be carried out before Allende was confirmed as president. An ex-Chilean brigadier general, Robert Viaux, was willing to lead such a mission but the commander of the Chilean Armed Forces, General René Schneider, did not approve of such an undemocratic undertaking. Despite Schneider's objections the CIA continued to plot with Viaux and two other conspirators, Colonel Paul Wimert, the US embassy's military attaché in Chile. and General Camillo Valenzuala, a Chilean army colonel. $50,000 was offered by the CIA for the abduction of Schneider, as well as tear gas and submachine guns. After two disastrous attempts the conspirators finally succeeded in removing Schneider on 23 October. The actual kidnap itself was

BELOW: President Allende (center) looks up as Chilean Air Force planes swoop over the presidential palace during the coup of 11 September 1973. Allende himself died in the coup, which followed months of mounting economic and political pressure, orchestrated by the CIA.

ABOVE: General Augusto Pinochet Ugarte, leader of the coup that overthrew Allende and iron-fisted ruler of Chile ever since. The undemocratic nature of Pinochet's rule has not unduly worried successive US administrations.

RIGHT: Suspected left-wingers rounded up after the coup were imprisoned in Chile's national stadium. There large numbers were tortured or murdered out of hand – one eye witness estimated that 500 prisoners were shot in the week after the coup.

unsuccessful, but wounds which Schneider sustained during the attempt were sufficient to end his life. The assassination of Schneider did not, though, prevent Allende from being confirmed as president. The assassination also did not stop Schneider's nominated successor, General Carlos Prats, becoming head of the Chilean military.

Immediately after Allende took up the office of president the CIA propaganda machine went into top gear. Journalists were commissioned to write anti-Allende articles. Even the prestigious US magazine *Time* was subverted when an article written by the Santiago correspondent which assessed that Allende did not present a communist threat to Latin America was changed to echo the contrary opinion after a CIA briefing. $3.5 million was pumped into the Chilean newspaper *El Mercurio* by the CIA between 1970 and 1973, and money was given to both the Christian Democrat Party and the right-wing National Party to allow them to buy newspapers and radio stations so they could step up the anti-Allende attack. It has been estimated that a total of $8 million was spent by the CIA to destabilize the Allende presidency.

On 11 September 1973 the CIA's efforts were at last successful. Allende died in a military coup led by General Augusto Pinochet Ugarte. Under Pinochet torture chambers were set up, political opposition was forbidden and thousands of Allende supporters were murdered. Officially the CIA did not overthrow Allende and yet if it had not pumped millions of dollars into the anti-Allende propaganda machine and into promoting strikes and other civil disturbances, it is reasonable to suppose that Pinochet and his right-wing henchmen would never have been able to seize power. It is also quite clear that Pinochet had been assured of US support for his action. One of the greatest ironies of the CIA interference in the affairs of Chile was that the Rockefeller Commission, set up to investigate the activities of the CIA, found that: 'There was never a significant threat of Soviet military presence in Chile; the export of Allende's revolution was limited and its value as a model more limited still.' Another Senate Committe found that the CIA had been responsible for 'weakening and, for the present time at least, an end to constitutional government in Chile.'

At an international level, the United States became the object of widespread criticism. While Pinochet's coup merely confirmed the suspicions of left-wing opponents of Western democracy, many of America's allies were shocked by the CIA's covert activities.

Since the fall of democracy in Chile, opposition to the regime has been restricted to illegal street demonstrations and sporadic guerrilla attacks, in the face of arbitrary imprisonment and torture. Attempts to resurrect a democratic opposition have been blocked by Pinochet's dedication to dictatorship. In 1986 guerrillas of the Movement of the Revolutionary Left came very close to assassinating Pinochet in a well-planned ambush, which suggested they might be more competent and better organized than previously suspected. It is still possible that the overthrow of Allende and democracy might in the end bring Chile the sort of revolutionary regime that the CIA most hoped to avoid.

ABOVE: A demonstrator against the Pinochet regime in 1986 is led away by riot police. The lack of democracy has radicalized opposition in Chile.

Toward the end of the 1970s, a new country came within the Soviet sphere of influence and thus qualified for treatment as part of the 'backyard': it was Afghanistan, a mountainous and underdeveloped state between the Soviet Union and Pakistan. In April 1978 a coup brought the pro-Soviet Noor Mohammed Taraki to power in Afghanistan and the Soviet Union, which had apparently played no part in Taraki's takeover, willingly responded to his request for advisors to assist in the Marxist transformation of the country. But Taraki's modernizing policies met with hostility from Afghanistan's mountain tribesmen, and the security situation worsened after September 1979, when Taraki's prime minister Hafizullah Amin seized power and killed the former president. With the tribal Muslim

The seizure of power in Afghanistan by Noor Mohammed Taraki (below) in April 1978 was followed by an invitation to Soviet advisors to move into the country. Taraki's successor, Hafizullah Amin (right), fell out with the Soviets when his extreme policies alienated the Afghan tribesmen and provoked a guerrilla uprising.

guerrillas, the Mujahidin, rampant, the Soviet Union faced the choice of withdrawing from Afghanistan or taking military action to maintain a pro-Soviet regime.

It has been suggested by some Soviet-watchers that the KGB was not in favor of the military option, but it must have played a full part in the execution of the invasion plan once it was decided. On 27 December 1979, Amin, who had refused either to invite the Soviet Army into Afghanistan or to resign, was killed by Soviet paratroopers storming his palace, while Soviet troops poured into the country. The bitter war against the Mujahidin increased in ferocity over the following years. Afghanistan rapidly became a center of intrigue and complex arms deals, with the CIA arming the rebel forces and the KGB supporting the Afghani government of the Soviet-installed Babrak Karmal.

Officially the United States is not involved in the Mujahidin struggle, but it is estimated that the CIA has supplied about $100 million in arms and ammunition to the rebels through contacts in Pakistan and the Middle East. When the war started most weapons for the Mujahidin came through Egypt to Pakistan. It now seems as if that source has dried up and weapons are being shipped from China to Pakistan and then smuggled into Afghanistan via the Pakistan Defence Ministry. The situation becomes very confusing when, according to one source: 'Russian-made arms captured by

The Soviet presence in Afghanistan at first consisted largely of a benign contribution to the country's development (left, a Soviet teacher at Kabul Polytechnic), but the mounting guerrilla war led to a massive military intervention that reduced much of Afghanistan to a wasteland of deserted villages and burnt-out crops (above, Soviet tanks parade through the capital, Kabul).

Israel from Syria and the PLO were sold to a Canadian middleman, then shipped through a US middleman to "somewhere in the Persian Gulf" and finally on to Pakistan and then passed across the Afghanistan border.'

One of the major roles which the KGB plays in the war is to seduce informers with the prospect of large rewards. This information can then be passed on to the Soviet military officers in command of the Soviet forces in Afghanistan. The Mujahidin have been lobbying Congress for an increase in US aid, arguing that the CIA effort is not efficient enough to achieve a lasting victory. But in 1986 the new Soviet administration under Premier Mikhail Gorbachev announced that the Soviet Union was to start a slow withdrawal of its forces from Afghanistan. It is interesting that the might of the Soviet Army and the KGB could not defeat groups of ill-equipped rebels fighting in loose guerrilla groups. If Gorbachev is as good as his word, then for the first time ever the Soviet Union would have conceded defeat in one of its 'backyard operations.'

WAR IN AFGHANISTAN

When the Soviet Army moved into Afghanistan in December 1979, they quickly discovered that they had taken on a formidable enemy. The Afghan tribesmen, forming the Islamic guerrilla force or Mujahidin, repeatedly humiliated Soviet troops in clashes in mountain terrain. But gradually the Soviets evolved more successful counter-insurgency techniques, both in the better use of suitable hardware such as helicopter gunships, and in psychological warfare masterminded by the KGB. A considerable number of Mujahidin were tempted onto the government side by a mixture of threats and rewards. And yet, the guerrillas – kept well supplied by the CIA and operating from safe bases in Pakistan – remained unsubdued, and in 1986 the Soviet Union announced the start of troop withdrawals from Afghanistan.

LEFT: An Afghan tribesman displays his Kalashnikov, probably obtained via a complex CIA-organized line of supply. BELOW, FAR LEFT: Mujahidin in triumph on top of a knocked-out Soviet armored personnel carrier. BELOW LEFT: Soviet infantry dismount from an armored column in difficult terrain. Soviet tactics improved noticeably as the war dragged on.

ABOVE: A Mujahidin leader and his colleagues in the Kunar Valley. The fearsome mountains of Afghanistan provided an excellent site for guerrilla warfare. LEFT: A young Afghan guerrilla in position for an ambush, with the ubiquitous AK-47.

RIGHT: A Soviet tank on the streets of Kabul. By 1987 Soviet troops were spending more of their time in their bases or the main cities, leaving the Afghan Army to fight the guerrillas in the mountains.

An operation which the Soviet Union would probably claim as a success was the action taken against the fledgling Polish free trade union Solidarnosč (Solidarity). Like Hungary, Poland had tried to modify the effects of Stalinism; the Poznan shipworkers had rebelled in 1956, and although this rebellion was quelled, it did have limited success in that a marginally more liberal regime was brought to power under a new leader, Wladyslaw Gomulka. In 1971, after a further period of discord, Gomulka was replaced by Edward Gierek. During the Gierek era, an obscure shipworker in the Baltic seaport of Gdynia, Lech Walesa, was becoming increasingly disaffected with the State-run trade union structure within Poland. He began exploring ways in which this structure could be changed in order to

act more efficiently and also how it could protect the workers against the State, rather than being dominated by the State. Together with other shipyard workers Lech Walesa founded the trade union Solidarity, the aims of which were to remain independent of State intervention and to bargain with the government over workers' rights. By the summer of 1981 Solidarity had grown in strength to encompass over two million members, some of whom were also members of Poland's Communist Party, including Walesa's deputy, Bogdan Lis.

As with both the Hungarian and Czech experiments, for a period censorship was relaxed. Film-maker Andrei Wajda was allowed to make a film for general release about the founding of the union, and the work of poet Czeslaw Milosz, for years

RIGHT: Lech Walesa, founder and leader of the Polish free trade union Solidarity. Before the creation of Solidarity, all the labor organizations in the country were under the direct control of the communist government and represented its wishes, rather than those of the union members.

LEFT: General Wojciech Jaruzelski, who took power in Poland in December 1981 and imposed martial law. Jaruzelski's regime was seen by Moscow as the only alternative to sending in the Soviet Army to re-establish its control.

BELOW: Polish peasants register their adherence to Solidarity. The movement embraced all elements of Polish society, both urban and rural.

ABOVE: Lech Walesa (right) with the outspoken pro-Solidarity priest Jerzy Popieluszko (center) who was later killed by members of the Polish secret police. The backing of the Catholic Church was essential to the success of Solidarity in marshalling mass support, and the Church had an even more important role to play after the suppression of the movement under martial law.

bers of the Polish Communist Party. Moscow, though, became increasingly perturbed with the direction that events were taking in Poland and on 13 December 1981 the world awoke to the news that overnight there had been a military takeover in Poland, under the leadership of general Wojciech Jaruzelski, a known hardliner. Within days Solidarity leaders had been arrested and imprisoned, including Walesa. The only vehicle of protest left was the church, and an attempt was made to close that avenue too with the kidnap and murder of an outspoken Warsaw priest named Jerzy Popieluszko. It was later discovered that Popieluszko had been murdered by members of the secret police. From 1981 to 1983 thousands of people were arrested and imprisoned under horrific conditions. Direct links with the KGB cannot be proved, yet it is evident that the secret police were extremely active during this time in surpressing any possible protest against the Moscow-backed Jaruzelski regime.

Meanwhile, the CIA continued to pursue its own 'backyard' policies. By the 1980s the focus was once more on Central America, with Nicaragua and El Salvador at the center of large-scale covert operations to protect American interests and political predominance. Clearly neither superpower intended to renounce its right to predominance in its own sphere, whatever the inhabitants of those regions might think.

considered too controversial, was suddenly heard to be read on State radio. Intellectual debate, with figures such as the radical Jacek Kuron participating, was also allowed. Solidarity was an enigma in that although there was mass support for the Catholic church from the trade union, always a strong facet of Polish life, the union also consisted of almost one million mem-

LEFT AND RIGHT: The unforgettable images of a peaceful popular revolt against Soviet domination in its East European 'backyard.'

CHAPTER 9

SPYING IN THE SEVENTIES

During the 1970s, the fate of the CIA and the KGB diverged. The American organization ran into a storm of public criticism as its most sordid operations were brought out into the daylight, while under the leadership of Yuri Vladimirovich Andropov, the KGB seemed to go from strength to strength.

When Andropov took over the KGB in 1967, the inefficiency of the massive organization was well attested. Denied control over Communist Party members by Khrushchev's reforms, from 1958 the KGB had been extensively restaffed with careerists from Komsomol, the communist youth organization. Aleksander Shelepin, who became chairman of the KGB in 1958, was the former secretary of the Komsomol central committee. The staff shake-up carried out by Shelepin filled the organization with people who had no experience of the secret service, and efficiency apparently suffered under him and his successor, Vladimir Yefimovich Semichastny. It was a time of

clumsiness and major intelligence setbacks. In 1962, for example, Colonel Oleg Penkovsky of Soviet military intelligence was arrested after he had been passing secrets to Britain's MI6 for almost two years. There was also the defection of Anatoli Golitsyn, a KGB agent working in Finland, who revealed the names of many Soviet agents in the West. And inside the Soviet Union, the rising dissident movement was badly mishandled, with the staging of show trials such as that of Sinyavsky and Daniel which turned into effective propaganda for the anti-Soviet movement, highlighting the crude injustice of Soviet repression.

Andropov had fought as a partisan behind German lines in World War II and in 1956 he had been Soviet ambassador to Hungary, although he had no diplomatic experience. It was widely believed that he became head of the KGB because of his actions in Hungary at the time of the uprising; he was involved in the arrange-

The period between 1961 and 1967 when Vladimir Semichastny (right) was head of the KGB saw a series of embarrassing setbacks for the Soviet secret service. None was worse than the revelation in 1962 that Colonel Oleg Penkovsky (on trial, above) had been a double agent, passing information to MI6 from inside Soviet military intelligence. The advent of Yuri Andropov (above right) as KGB chief brought a new professionalism to the service, improving its success rate and its public image in the Soviet Union.

ment of the fatal dinner party at which General Maleter was arrested. When it became known that Andropov had been appointed chairman of the KGB, operators in the field were overjoyed because, in the words of Arkady Shevchencko, 'at last we have got a strong man as our chief.' Andropov restored order to the KGB ranks, forbade drinking and increased the organization's foreign agent power by raising the status of KGB agents working within Soviet embassies abroad. The quality of agents was also improved – they had everything from better-tailored suits to better foreign languages – and Andropov is also credited with the reorganization of the KGB.

The KGB has a massive staff: there are estimated to be 90,000 staff officers, as well as 300,000 border guards and a further 100,000 clerical workers, building guards and special troops. The headquarters, known as the Center, are at 2 Dzerzhinsky Square in the heart of Moscow, close to the

145

Despite the secretiveness of Soviet society, the KGB has a relatively high profile. Its old headquarters in Dzerzhinsky Square (above) is a prominent landmark in central Moscow, and KGB troops (right) are clearly identified by their distinctive military uniforms.

Kremlin. Part of the Center is made up of the remains of the notorious Lubyanka prison. To join the KGB, one is summoned; applications are not seriously considered. Most members are nominated by other KGB officers or chosen from relatives of officers.

Three of the KGB's four Chief Directorates are devoted to domestic affairs. In this the KGB differs sharply from the CIA, which is not legally entitled to carry out operations inside the United States (although it has been known to do so). The Second Chief Directorate is responsible for internal security in general, with powers of surveillance over both Soviet citizens and foreigners in the Soviet Union. Much of its work involves trying to compromise or otherwise recruit foreign journalists or embassy staff. The use of sexual blackmail as a technique increased under Andropov. In 1968 the British ambassador to Moscow, Sir Geoffrey Harrison, was seduced by his chambermaid. On realizing the implications Harrison confessed the matter to his superiors at the Foreign Office and was recalled. Interestingly, Harrison allowed

embassy in search of references, he suggested that Galia was not the most ideal of employees.

In 1981 two US military attachés in Moscow were accused of sexual misconduct. The two men, Major James R Holbrook and Lieutenant Colonel Thomas Spencer, were accused by the Soviet authorities of sexual misbehavior in the Ukrainian town of Rovno. The attachés left the Soviet Union, but not before the CIA had accused the Soviets of deliberately blackmailing the men. That the practice continues became evident in 1987 when a scandal broke concerning the sexual misconduct of US Marines stationed with diplomatic missions in the Soviet Union.

In 1969 Andropov created the Fifth Chief Directorate specifically to deal with dissidents, who were otherwise the responsibility of the Second Chief Directorate. It is generally agreed that the new ways of dealing with dissidents that were then evolved played a large part in limiting the growth and influence of the dissident movement. The KGB did everything in its power to avoid trials which would provide the dissidents with a propaganda platform and create a focus for international sympathy. Instead, covert pressure was mounted on dissidents at home or at their place of work in an attempt to force them either to renounce their activities or to choose exile in the West. In the case of more recalcitrant opponents of the regime, psychiatric hospitals were increasingly used as an alternative to imprisonment, with dissidence defined as a form of mental illness.

ABOVE: Sir Geoffrey Harrison, who had to leave his post as British Ambassador to Moscow after being seduced by a KGB agent. RIGHT: Dissident Vladimir Bukovsky who came to the West in a 'swap' for Chilean communist leader Luis Corvalan in 1976.

himself to become seduced by 'Galia' even though every diplomat embarking on an overseas mission is warned of the perils of such compromising situations. Harrison resumed his duties in London, but Galia was kept on at the Moscow embassy in order not to reveal that her cover had been blown. The incoming ambassador Sir Duncan Wilson retained her services and then fired her after six weeks. Undeterred, Galia then approached the Australian embassy in search of a job. When a somewhat bemused Wilson was contacted by the Australian

LEFT: Dissident Soviet Jew Anatoly Shcharansky (center) walks across the Glienecker Bridge in Berlin, freed as part of a prisoner exchange in 1986. Since the 1970s it has been Soviet policy to transfer the most intransigent dissidents to the West, weakening the dissident movement inside the Soviet Union and removing a focus for anti-Soviet propaganda.

BELOW: Andrei Sakharov, nuclear physicist and critic of the Soviet regime. In 1986 the Soviet government tried to achieve a reconciliation with Sakharov, possibly keen to use his talents in developing their own version of 'star wars' technology.

RIGHT: The KGB in action. Alexander Podrabinek, member of a committee investigating the use of psychiatric treatment against opponents of the Soviet regime, is arrested by the secret police in April 1977. It was convenient for the Soviet Union to label dissidents as insane, so they could be locked up and 'treated' without the need for a trial.

When cases did come to court, evidence was competently presented and the letter of Soviet law apparently observed to minimize the grounds for criticism. Increasingly the most prominent dissidents either chose to live in the West or were deported there and by 1980 the movement within the Soviet Union was far weaker than it had been a decade earlier.

The third section of the KGB operating within the Soviet Union was the Border Guards Chief Directorate. It is another major distinction between the KGB and the CIA that the Soviet organization is for a large part military, where the CIA is entirely civilian. The KGB includes not only the Border Guards but also various special forces that operate in close liaison with the Soviet Army. These include troops stationed in various frontier areas that speak the language of the country across the border, offering clear advantages for certain types of military intervention. By the 1970s, the traditional hostility between the Soviet Army and the secret police that had characterized Stalin's time had mostly disappeared. Andropov was careful to encourage co-operation between the KGB and the Army, both in intelligence and in active operations, and his successor Vitali Fedorchuck ordered that KGB staff officers should normally wear uniform – they were not to be seen as a secret police force but as

a military formation. This is typical of the KGB's concern to improve its image inside the Soviet Union. To the same end, feature films were promoted in which KGB agents played an heroic role, sometimes almost in the James Bond mold.

The supposedly glamorous side of the KGB's business, external espionage, is handled by the First Chief Directorate. Its various tasks include standard intelligence gathering, the penetration of foreign governments and security services, support for friendly guerrilla movements and liaison with the security services of the East European 'satellite states' and Cuba. The 11th Department of the First Chief Directorate is specifically responsible for contacts with these 'friendly' security services, and offers them training and equipment.

Although some KGB agents abroad are 'illegals' living unobtrusive lives under assumed names, like George Lonsdale or Rudolf Abel, and others are double agents like Philby, the vast majority are openly attached to Soviet embassies or other Soviet organizations like the airline Aeroflot or press agencies. This is not very different from the way the CIA or MI6 operates, but the numbers of KGB agents are considerably higher. A French security official once stated: 'Of approximately 1000 Soviet bloc representatives in France in 1971, 600 were professional espionage officers; to maintain complete surveillance over so large a group is an enormous, if not impossible, task.'

Mass expulsions of Soviet diplomats identified as spies has become a regular feature of international life – they cannot be arrested, of course, enjoying diplomatic immunity. One of the most dramatic of all spy expulsions took place in London in 1971. To the astonishment of the British, in the fall of 1971 Conservative Prime Minister Edward Heath announced that 90 Soviet diplomats were to be expelled for 'subversive and espionage activities against the United Kingdom' and a further 15 diplomats, who at that time were out of the country, were also to join their comrades on the journey home. The expulsion of the diplomats stemmed from the defection of Oleg Lyalin, a KGB officer who had posed as a member of the Soviet trade mission to

ligence sources estimated that 36 percent of all Soviet officials stationed in Western European embassies were spies.

Another area in which the KGB's First Chief Directorate excels is that of deliberate disinformation. When Joseph Frolik defected from the Czech secret service in 1969, he proceeded to make the most astonishing allegations concerning leading members of the British parliament. Intelligence officers now believe that Frolik's book *The Frolik Defection* is very probably a disinformation plant, guaranteed to occupy the time of security officers and thus distract them from carrying out more serious work. Journalists have often been used as spies or to mount disinformation campaigns. One of the most highly successful was Vitali Yevgennevich Lui, otherwise known as Victor Louis, who worked for the London

BELOW AND BELOW LEFT: The seemingly innocent facade of Soviet espionage. The Moscow Narodny Bank in the City of London and the Soviet trade mission building housed some of the 105 spies exposed in 1971 when Oleg Lyalin, a KGB officer attached to the mission, defected.

Britain. Lyalin claimed that the 105 had been involved in an immense program destined to cause havoc in Britain. Included in the plans was a Soviet attack on British radar stations and communications facilities. Lyalin claimed that he was personally to be involved in the destruction of the Early Warning Monitoring Station at Fylingdales in North Yorkshire. Other plans which Lyalin revealed suggested that the Soviets were prepared to flood the London Underground system. He reported to MI6 that teams of British traitors had been recruited by the KGB and were simply waiting for the command to put their instructions into effect. Later evidence has shown that Lyalin may have become more than slightly carried away and it is now believed that most of the 105 were involved in illegal trade transactions centered around Britain's electronics industry. In 1971 the Soviets, despite having been the first nation in space, still badly needed more information about the West's progress with computers. Further to these revelations, in 1972 Western intel-

ABOVE: Yasser Arafat, chairman of the PLO, has survived two decades of struggle against Israel and against Palestinian rivals. The Soviet Union's support for the PLO is often cited as an example of the KGB backing terrorism, but the Soviets have always distanced themselves from the terrorist side of PLO activities.

Evening News in the 1950s. Others can only be recognized by behavior not to be expected of a journalist. When *Pravda* assigned its chief foreign correspondent, Vladimir Gregorovich, to the Philippines in 1974, it was seen as 'rather an obscure posting for a distinguished journalist.' Since Gregorovich also filed no copy, it can only be assumed he was not there to get news stories. By the same token, observing that the Soviet Union has no less than seven correspondents in India, compared to Reuters' two, it is easy to suspect that they are in fact gathering information of various kinds for the KGB.

The First Chief Directorate's role in connection with guerrilla and, it has been alleged, terrorist organizations is the subject of much controversy. Certainly, the KGB has been involved in providing both arms and training for what it regards as 'liberation movements,' either directly as in the case of the Palestine Liberation Organi-

zation (PLO) or indirectly as in Latin America, where the Cuban security services have been the intermediary. The Soviet Union has always denied aiding 'terrorists,' however, an attitude many of its enemies regard with extreme skepticism. Some have gone so far as to see Moscow as the hub of a worldwide terror network, unifying such diverse movements as the Irish Republican Army (IRA), the Baader-Meinhof gang and the Sandinistas. Part of the answer, of course, is that one man's terrorist is another man's freedom fighter. The Soviet Union openly supports the PLO but does not regard it as a terrorist organization; the Israelis and the United States do. From Palestinian accounts it would seem clear that both the training and equipment provided by the Soviets have been directed toward conventional or guerrilla war, rather than the hijacking of aircraft or the planting of bombs in airports. The Soviet Union has toyed with backing the IRA, providing arms through Czechoslovakia, but no very serious connection appears to exist.

More serious is the accusation that the KGB has backed pure terrorists with no possible claim to be 'liberation movements' of any kind. The famous 'Carlos,' born Ilich Ramirez Sanchez, who became the most wanted international terrorist of the 1970s, certainly spent a year at Moscow's Patrice Lumumba University in 1968, and it is quite possible that his expulsion from the Soviet Union after only a year, apparently for dissolute behavior, was a KGB ploy to divert suspicion from a man who was now their agent. Yet no really firm evidence of KGB backing for Carlos has come to light. Again, convoluted plots have been constructed linking the KGB with the attempted assassination of Pope John Paul II in 1981. The would-be assassin, Mohammed Ali Agca, apparently claimed to have been acting on behalf of the Bulgarian security services, presumably themselves under the instructions of a KGB wishing to rid itself of a turbulent priest. But Agca has since withdrawn his allegations against the Bulgarians, and the matter remains totally obscure. The observer of these events is doubly disadvantaged in that not only are the KGB bound to lie about their involvement, but the only other sources of information, the Western security services, are equally likely to be pushing 'disinformation.'

To return to Andropov, his reorganization of the KGB created a system in which the four Chief Directorates centralized power within the organization, thus giving the chairman very effective control over its

ABOVE AND LEFT: The IRA showing off for the cameras. Despite Eastern bloc support for the Irish Republicans, their main source of arms and money has remained consistently the United States, despite all the efforts of the US government to stop its citizens contributing such aid.

Despite its popular image in the West as a gar
callous terrorists, the Palestine Liberation
Organization (PLO) is regarded in other parts c
world as a heroic body of freedom fighters pur
the just cause of a Palestinian homeland. The S
Union has backed the PLO since the 1960s, an
KGB has organized training courses in the Sovi
Union as well as supplying arms and equipmen
the Soviets have distanced themselves from PL
terrorist activities, such as plane hijacks, encou
more conventional tactics. The rout of the PLO
Israeli invasion of Lebanon (June 1982) cast sor
doubt on the wisdom of Soviet policy – the PLO'
Soviet tanks and artillery were overwhelmed by
Israeli armed forces.

ABOVE: The stern face of
the PLO. TOP RIGHT: PLO
chief Yasser Arafat (center
eft) meets Soviet leader
Yuri Andropov (second
from right). During
Andropov's period in
control of the KGB, the
Soviet Union consistently
backed the PLO in its war
against Israel.

ABOVE, LEFT AND FAR LEFT: PLO recruits undergo training at one of their desert camps. The KGB encouraged this sort of military preparation, designed for guerrilla raids across the Israeli border or for a confrontation with Israel in conventional war. Soviet principles of warfare and Soviet equipment proved totally inadequate, however, in the face of the highly sophisticated Israeli Defense Force.

multifarious activities. It was said that at some stage of every KGB operation, Andropov knew exactly what was going on. He used his powerful instrument to create a strong political base for himself within the Soviet system. One of the main preoccupations of the 'domestic' side of the KGB under Andropov was to attack corruption in the Communist Party itself. Khrushchev's success in excluding the KGB from power over party members was largely reversed. Some of the anti-corruption campaigns were spectacular, especially in Azerbaijan in 1969 and in Georgia in 1971. By 1980, Soviet leader Leonid Brezhnev and his close circle of friends and relatives were under attack from the KGB for corruption. It is not surprising that Andropov, a member of the ruling Politburo since 1973, should have emerged as Soviet leader in 1982, after Brezhnev's death.

If the KGB exerted itself to attack the politically powerful in the Soviet Union in the 1970s, the CIA by contrast found itself under attack by American politicians,

accused of illegal operations and the uncontrolled exercise of power. The first blow for the Agency came in 1973 when director Richard Helms, who since his appointment in 1966 had presided over a series of controversial operations in Laos, Cambodia, South Vietnam, Chile and elsewhere, was actually fired from office rather than leaving voluntarily. The firing of Helms did not spring from a US love of justice and worry about these overseas missions, many of which had ended in disaster, however. It was ordered by President Richard Nixon who was embroiled in one of the largest domestic scandals ever to hit the United States – Watergate. Watergate was surprisingly one of the few murky areas where Helms refused to allow the Agency to become involved. As a consequence, he was summoned to Camp David by Nixon and informed that his services as director of the CIA were no longer required. Subsequently he was offered the post of ambassador to Iran. Some commentators allege that Helms was offered the position out of fear, as Nixon

BELOW: A false passport belonging to Iliich Ramon Sanchez, better known as the international terrorist 'Carlos.' Perhaps Carlos's most spectacular action was the kidnapping of 11 OPEC ministers, representing all the major Arab oil states, in December 1975.

was worried that Helms might release information about the Watergate break-in. Others have suggested that Helms blackmailed Nixon into giving him the post. Helms has always denied the blackmail allegations: 'I certainly did not blackmail Nixon. Of all the accusations made about me and my leadership of the CIA I have resented none more than the charge I blackmailed Nixon.'

An important fact about Helms, which possibly explains a little about this complex and difficult person, is that he wholeheartedly believed that everything he did while director of the Agency he also did for the greater good of the United States. At a rare speaking engagement in 1971 Helms went on the record, saying: 'The nation must to a degree take it on faith that we, too, are honorable men devoted to her service.'

Helms' background was similar to that of many successful CIA operatives. He had studied in Switzerland and Germany and had later graduated from St Williams College in 1935. He then went to work as a

ABOVE: James R Schlesinger was briefly director of the CIA between the departure of Richard Helms in February 1973 and the arrival of William Colby the following July. Another notable US politician to serve a short spell as CIA chief was George Bush, who filled the post for three months in 1976.

RIGHT: President Nixon dismissed CIA director Helms in 1973 before meeting his own downfall in the Watergate scandal. Watergate in turn led to a hostile public investigation of the CIA, especially by a Senate committee chaired by Senator Frank Church.

journalist on the *Indianapolis Times*, after which the war broke out and Helms served as a Navy lieutenant commander attached to the OSS. Helms stayed on after the war in the CIA, a rapidly rising star. By 1959 he was in a senior enough position to have full knowledge of the CIA's efforts to have Castro assassinated. At a 1975 Senate Intelligence Committee hearing Helms said of the matter that he fully believed in those attempts, some involving Mafia leaders, and that the CIA was 'acting within the scope of its authority.'

This was not a widely shared conviction, however, as revelations about CIA activities tumbled out in the mid-1970s. Under William Colby, who succeeded to the directorship of the Agency in July 1973, agents were instructed to reveal all they knew about past CIA operations that might be illegal or were previously unacknowledged. In the mood generated by Watergate, when the lifting of the secrecy surrounding government seemed the highest public duty, the Senate's Church Committee and the Rockefeller Commission dug unsparingly into the Agency's darkest corners. It was revealed that under President Nixon, the CIA had operated extensively in the United States, penetrating the anti-Vietnam War movement and other radical organizations, and carrying out a wide range of other activities connected with surveillance and intelligence gathering, in direct violation of the law which restricted its operations to foreign targets. Operation Chaos, the codename for this domestic espionage, had been organized by James Angleton, whose career was broken by the revelations. All the now familiar truths about the attempted assassinations of foreign heads of state and destabilization of democratically-elected governments shocked the American public, who had heard their political leaders deny such facts many times over in the past. Helms himself was eventually found guilty of lying to a Senate Foreign Relations Committee – he had asserted that there had been no CIA destabilization of Chile – and sentenced to a fine and a two-year suspended prison term.

Congress was determined to control US foreign policy and set about subjecting CIA operations to a series of oversight commit-

tees. With the election of Jimmy Carter as President in 1976, the humiliation of the Agency was soon complete. Carter appointed Admiral Stansfield Turner to head the CIA in 1977, with a specific brief to curtail and control its activities. The number of operatives was cut from several thousand to just 300. Covert operations were reduced to two or three a year and the International Activists Division (a special covert action unit) was reduced to a shadow of its former importance. The whole emphasis of the CIA's work was shifted to electronic espionage, using the latest and best technology. The 'old hands' with their often ramshackle clandestine operations mounted with loosely supervised multi-million dollar budgets were definitely out. By the end of the 1970s, the CIA budget was only 40 percent of its level at the start of the decade and its total workforce had been halved. In a reversal of earlier years, America's allies had become unwilling to share secrets with the Agency, since the insistence on 'open government' meant that the secrets could almost certainly not be kept. And yet President Ronald Reagan and a new era for the CIA were just around the corner.

LEFT: President Jimmy Carter was committed to open government and a principled foreign policy. Under his administration, CIA activities were severely curtailed and old-style 'cloak-and-dagger' operations went out of fashion.

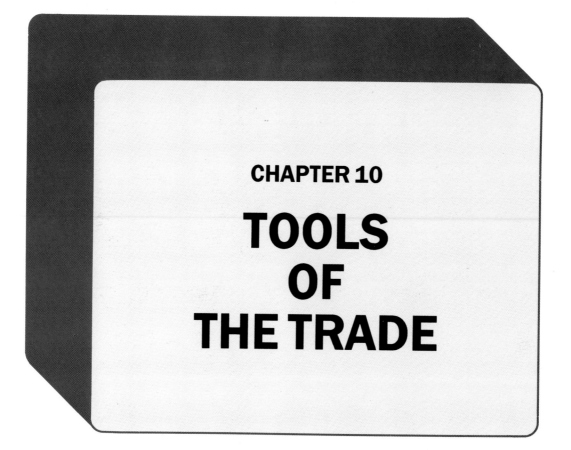

CHAPTER 10

TOOLS
OF
THE TRADE

From the earliest days of espionage, secrecy and disguise have played a role of paramount importance, points taken a little too seriously at Truman's 'cloak and dagger' party of 1946. It is, after all, a fairly sensible premise that if one wishes to seek information from someone who does not want to give it, then inevitably devious methods will have to be employed to gain that information. Sometimes of course, methods of deception and secrecy are not only used to gain information; on some occasions these methods are also used for murder and assassination.

A major operation involving deception and poison concerned the Bulgarian secret service and a Bulgarian exile named Georgi Markov. In 1978 Markov, an emigré employee of Radio Free Europe, was walking near the BBC World Service offices in London's Aldwych when he suddenly felt a sharp pain in his leg. On turning round to see what had caused this pain, Markov

Defector riddle deepens
MI5 HUNT 'POISON BROLLY KILLER'

MRS ANNABEL MARKOV—being very brave and talking to detectives at her home today.

By John Stevens and Patrick McGowan

MI5 AND Scotland Yard's Anti Ter-rorist Branch this afternoon joined forces in investigating the death of George Markov the Bulgarian defec-tor who died a week after he was jab-bed with the point of a possibly pois-oned umbrella.

A post mortem on Mr Markov, 49, today, was inconclusive. But the possibility that he was mur-dered by an East European agent has not been ruled out.

And the fact that the Secret Service, the Yard's Anti-Terrorist Branch and the Special Branch are all now actively engaged on the investigation does nothing to weaken it.

Mr Markov was a broadcaster with the BBC's Overseas Service. He had feared for his life ever since he settled in Britain seven years ago, colleagues say.

He died yesterday, a week after telling his wife that he had been jabbed in the back of the thigh with an umbrella while standing in a bus queue at the Aldwych.

He developed a high temperature on the night after he returned home.

There was a mark on Mr Markov's body which COULD have been caused by an umbrella.

At the end of the 90-minute post mortem examin-ation Dr Rufus Compton, Home Office pathologist, was unable to say for certain what caused Mr Mar-kov's death.

And Commander James Nevill, head of the Anti-Terrorist Branch, said after the examination: "It has not revealed the cause of death—it does not seem to be from natural causes at this stage."

Said Commander Nevill: "We are dealing with it as a death caused under suspicious circumstances although there is no indication at this stage of how it was caused.

"Certain matters have been said which leave an area of doubt as to the possible cause of death."

Now a number of specimens from Mr Markov's body have been taken away for examination by forensic scientists at Scotland Yard's laboratory in Lambeth.

It may be several days before the results are known.

Mr Peter Fraenkel, head of the BBC's East Euro-pean service for which Mr Markov worked, said this afternoon Mr Markov had spoken to friends of threats to kill him. And he was worried about the possibilit yof being kidnapped.

Mr Markov's wife, Annabel, was today talking to detectives at her home in Lynette Avenue, Clapham.

Her brother, Mr Fisher Dilke, said: "She is being very brave indeed about the whole thing and is bear-ing up very well."

LEFT: A newspaper report on the mysterious death of Bulgarian exile Georgi Markov (far left), killed by a poisoned pellet that may have been carried on the ferrule of an umbrella. The murderer has never been identified, but it was the Bulgarian secret service that wanted Markov dead.

spotted a man of foreign appearance run-ning away from the scene.

Later that evening Markov developed a fever and the next day he was admitted to hospital. Three days later he died. An examination of his body revealed a circular area of inflammation on the right thigh with a central puncture mark about two milli-meters in diameter. On closer examination it was perceived that beneath the victim's skin there was a spherical piece of metal made of a platinum/iridium alloy which is used mainly in the aircraft industry, pierced with four tiny holes. A scientist who gave evidence at the inquest suggested that such an object could only be made with the aid of

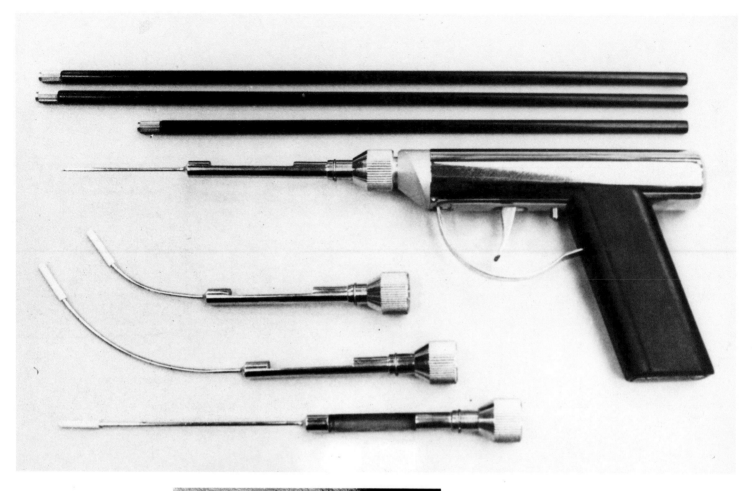

ABOVE: A gun for firing poison pellets, perhaps the kind of weapon used to kill Markov. The barrel would have been removed and concealed inside the umbrella, with a special firing mechanism.

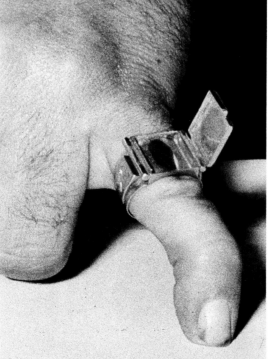

RIGHT: A ring with a secret cavity, used by espionage agents for carrying microfilm or, conceivably, a cyanide capsule.

a high-temperature furnace and precision drilling equipment. The conclusion of the inquest was that Markov had been killed by the introduction of poison into his bloodstream by means of this pellet. The murderer was never traced.

The Markov story brought other similar cases to light, most of which are believed to have been carried out by the Bulgarian secret service. In July 1973 a Bulgarian exile Boris Arnoff disappeared from his home in Aarhus, Denmark. Shortly afterward he appeared before a court in Sofia, the capital of Bulgaria, charged with anti-State activity. He was sentenced to 15 years imprisonment and actually died in prison a couple of months after this sentence commenced. A warning article was then published in the Bulgaria Communist Youth magazine *Narodna Mladeh* which briefly detailed the crimes that this so-called traitor had carried out. The article also stated that 'the same fate awaits anyone who forgets the ideals of the fatherland.'

In August 1978 Vladimir Kostov, a Bulgarian exile domiciled in Paris, was leaving the metro with his wife when he felt a sharp pain in his thigh. A high fever followed, which after three days, eventually burned itself out and allowed Kostov to recover. After the Markov case had been publicized, Kostov went for a medical examination. The results of an X-ray revealed a small metal object. London detectives flew to Paris and in their presence a surgeon removed the particle of metal from the thigh. When the particle was placed under a microscope it was seen to be identical to the object which had contained the poison that killed Markov. On further examination scientists

the questions to be asked, and the subject is then wired up. A corrugated rubber tube is placed around the chest to measure breathing, a blood pressure cuff is fixed around the arm, and a hand-held device is put in the hand to register any changes of electrical resistance of the skin, due to perspiration. All responses are traced by means of a graph. An initial series of control questions are asked to which it is known that the subject is giving the right answers, and then the real tests start. The graph should register any irregularities which occur and the subject is asked why that particular question caused problems. A second test then ensues – usually a total of four tests are taken – after which the subject is informed of the results. Polygraph tests also bring out other psychological traits, such as the subjects ability to cope under stress. In Britain, though, the polygraph has met with considerable resistance. GCHQ wanted to give all of its employees polygraph tests, but the employees resisted any such moves. Their resistance was mainly based on assertions that the polygraph is of limited value; some technical experts believe that the psychological stresses which the machine records can be caused by other factors and therefore should not be used as the sole determining test in employee vetting procedures. The use of the polygraph has now spread to

Two types of lie detector: the Voice Stress Analyzer (left) and the more elaborate polygraph machine (above) that measures changes in heartbeat rate, respiration and the surface of the skin. The use of lie detectors is highly controversial, with many critics claiming they are neither accurate nor reliable.

decided that the poison which had been used was probably ricin, an extremely toxic substance derived from castor oil.

To carry out checks on its own workers as well as to test evidence from other sources, both the KGB and the CIA use the lie detector or polygraph. The standard polygraph records physiological changes which are caused by stress, excitement and emotional reactions. Other general body changes which are recorded include blood pressure, perspiration levels and body temperature. These changes are all noted while the subject answers a series of Yes/No questions. A standard question which the CIA used was: 'Have you stolen any government property?,' to which the subject usually registered an abnormal response. An initial interview is set up to run through

commercial life and it is known that many of the world's major banks use the machine for testing employee security status.

Control of the mind has fascinated both agencies, though hard evidence of Soviet involvement in these tests is hard to come by. The first CIA attempt to discover the ultimate mind-control drug started in 1950 and was called Bluebird; other names followed such as Mkultra. When Richard Helms was deputy director of plans he suggested to director Allen Dulles that $300,000 be put toward funding research in chemical and biological materials. Dulles approved the project and it was put under the control of chemist Sidney Gottlieb. Universities' chemistry labs, hospitals and research bodies were all used in the search and a number of front organizations were also set up. These included the Society for the Investigation of Human Ecology, the Scientific Engineering Institute and also two funding organizations, the Josiah Macy Jnr Foundation and the Geschickter Fund for

Medical Research. The United States claimed that the Soviet Union was also practicing mind control, and cited dazed victims of the Stalin show trials as evidence, as well as confused prisoners returning home from the Korean War. A CIA memo from the chief of medical staff dated January 1952 states: 'there is ample evidence in the reports of innumerable interrogations that the communists were utilizing drugs, physical duress, electric shock and possibly hypnosis against their enemies. We are

forced by the mounting evidence to assume a more aggressive role in the development of these techniques, but must be cautious to maintain strict inviolable control because of the havoc that could be wrought by such techniques in unscrupulous hands.'

The first president of the World Psychiatric Association, Dr Ewen Cameron, was an early enthusiastic experimenter. Cameron experimented with the drugs Thorazine, Nembutal, Seconal, Veronal and Pheneregan, to see if he could 'wipe clean' patients' minds. The patient, under the influence of these drugs, would sleep for 30-day periods, during which a tape recorder would be placed under the patient's pillow with recordings continually repeating the same message. The Agency wished to discover if it were possible to reprogram a brain. Donald Hebb, McGill University's psychology professor, said of these highly dubious experiments that: 'If you actually look at what he was doing and wrote what he wrote, it would make you laugh. If I had a

LSD or 'Acid' became world famous as a drug used by young people in the late 1960s to 'expand consciousness' and achieve a mystical experience. Psychologist Timothy Leary (below) advocated the drug's use as a universal palliative, and his disciples were soon dishing out the pills (right). But the CIA had examined other possible uses of LSD over a decade earlier.

graduate student who talked like that, I'd throw him out.'

Sensory deprivation was also tested. The patient was immobilized by the same poison which South American Indians use to tip their arrows. Then he was cut off from all external stimulus for a long period of time. The experiment was later recorded as a failure, but other versions of sensory deprivation have been used in interrogation since, especially in Northern Ireland in 1971 when British security forces tried out the method on interned Irish Catholics.

The National Institute of Mental Health's Addiction Research Center at Lexington, Kentucky, also became involved in the CIA's experiments. Under its director Dr Harris Isabell the Center tested scopolamine, rivea seed and bufonteine as well as the now infamous lysergic acid diethylamide, otherwise known as LSD. During one early experiment with LSD Isabell recorded the effects on seven subjects of a trip lasting for 77 days. Isabell's report, among others, convinced the CIA that the drug was the one which it wanted to work with and encouraged the Agency to carry out further experiments at the University of Illinois Medical School, the University of Oklahoma, the Mount Sinai Hospital and Columbia University, New York. Gottlieb instructed Mount Sinai to carry out experiments on behalf of the Agency, in the areas of behavior disturbance, changes of sex patterns and the creation of dependence. Some of these tests were the precursors for Gottlieb's experiments to find a drug to alter the behavior of Fidel Castro.

At Fort Derrick the Agency experimented with germ warfare. Further experimentation, carried out in 1953, involved the testing of LSD. Seventy micrograms were put into a bottle of Cointreau, a glass of which was given to an unsuspecting civilian, Dr Frank Olsen. After a while the drug started to take an effect on Olsen who became very lively and animated; this artificial state of euphoria did not last and later that evening Olsen became deeply depressed and expressed a desire to see a psychiatrist. This was forbidden since the CIA did not wish to have their experimentation jeopardized. Eventually, though, the Agency found a doctor who had sufficient security clearance to examine Olsen. The doctor whom the CIA had chosen was Dr Harold Abramson, a Mount Sinai immunologist – not a qualified psychologist. Olsen met Abramson for a series of treatments, none of which cleared up his depression. Four days later (27 November) Olsen crashed through the window of the Washington Statler Hotel

and died instantly on the pavement. Any police investigation was forbidden. The Olsen family only found out the truth about what had gone on in 1975 when the Rockefeller Committee revealed the true circumstances of Olsen's death. The actual LSD projects – codenamed Mkultra – did not stop until 1963. Other experiments with narcotics and poisons continued. These included experiments in germ warfare and also experiments with bacteria based on tropical diseases.

The Soviet Union also became obsessed with mind-conditioning drugs and treatments. As well as being involved in assassination attempts in the outside world, one of the more notorious features of the KGB was its experimentation on Soviet dissidents within Soviet psychiatric hospitals and jails. The Lubyanka even has a special isolation unit for this purpose. Perfectly healthy patients are treated with very strong drugs, usually used for people suffering from a severe psychotic disorder, in an effort to weaken the prisoner's morale to such an extent that he or she becomes an acquiescent vegetable. An Amnesty International report listed the Serbsky Institute in Moscow and the Oryol Special Hospital as two of the places where these hideous experiments have taken place.

ABOVE: An LSD trip in progress. It was agreed by all users of the drug that it had to be taken in the right, peaceful conditions. But the CIA experimented on individuals who had no idea what was happening to them, and in at least one case this resulted in suicide.

A USAF Atlas-Agena space-booster blasts a VELA nuclear detection satellite into orbit (below), while technicians inspect a communications satellite prior to launch (below right).
RIGHT: A satellite's view of the world, looking down over Alaska.

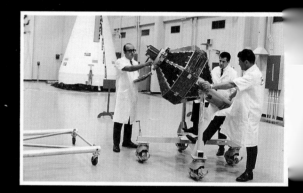

Prior to the development of powerful satellite surveillance systems, the two main sources of intelligence about a potential enemy came from the activities of spies (and other similar intelligence gatherers) and from strategic reconnaissance aircraft. The modern satellite has virtually superceded the high-flying aircraft and complements the traditional work of the spy. From its high vantage point (safe from territorial injunctions — unlike Powers' U2, for example) the military satellite can accurately photograph vast areas of the landscape below and yet can monitor details as small as the movement of individual soldiers. In addition, the satellite is able to pick up the conversations of tank commanders on the ground. It is these remarkable powers of intelligence gathering that makes the satellite such an important tool in the armory of the CIA and KGB.

LEFT: A satellite picture of the Dead Sea and the River Jordan, a key strategic area for detailed surveillance from space. A US Challenger Space Shuttle blasts off with a defense satellite on board (below), while an operational defense satellite begins its orbit (below left).

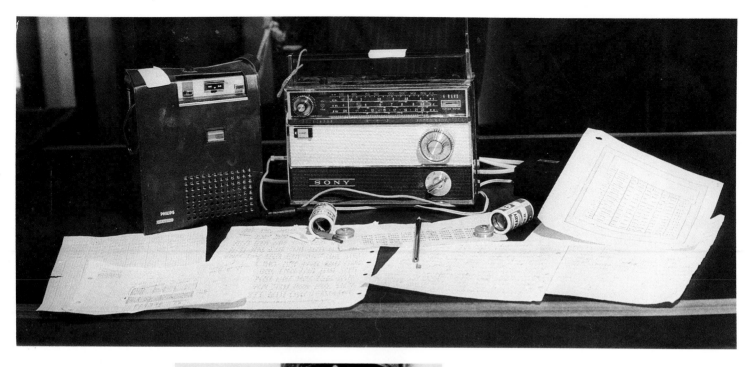

The equipment of Soviet spies caught in Britain: a 1971 raid on a house in London revealed (above) a shortwave radio and recorder, a code sheet, hollowed-out torch batteries for concealing film, and an apparently ordinary pencil that could be unscrewed to provide another hiding place. The 'one-time pad' (right), a list of personal codes, belonged to a British air force technician who spied for the Soviets in the 1960s.

Some of the tools of espionage are so fantastic that they would appear to have come straight from the pages of a James Bond movie, rather than actually to have been used in time of peace against an enemy of the intelligence agencies. Spies working undercover in a foreign country need to receive instructions from their masters, and one of the devices used to this end is a 'one-time pad.' The 'one-time pad' is small enough to be disguised in a cigarette packet. Basically it consists of lists of an agent's personal ciphers. These ciphers or codes are just lists of numbers thrown out at random by a computer. When the controller wishes to contact a particular agent these codes are read out in a specific order. Agents from the Eastern bloc often receive their orders or numbers from shortwave radio transmitters or on some occasions on the shortwave band of a domestic radio. In Europe if you tune into the East German stations on the shortwave band late at night lists of numbers can often be heard being read out. These numbers are instructing a specific agent to check the sequences in his/her pad and then translate the sequence with their own cipher. Another way of communicating with agents who use one-time pads is through the medium of personal advertisements in daily newspapers; some of the classified ads take on a very different meaning if the reader knows what to look for. In Britain it has long been suspected that a favored publication is the *Daily Telegraph.* Short of checking up on all the answerbacks, the casual reader will never really know if the message is 'spooked' or not.

A spy who excelled at this type of undercover work was the Soviet agent Boris Animisovich Skoridov. Skoridov used the operational name Ivan and was originally based at the Soviet embassy in London. In 1959 Skoridov was sent to Australia where he assumed the functions of First Secretary of the embassy. It has been alleged that his real mission was to re-establish a Soviet undercover network in the country. Letters have since been found which revealed that Skoridov made great use of invisible ink. The documents initially looked like ordinary letters written to a friend, but unfortunately for Skoridov the recipient of his letters was an Australian double agent who was able to pass on this mail to her superiors in Melbourne. By treating the letters with a special chemical solution a totally different message was revealed, usually asking his contact to meet him and exchange packages with him.

Another tried-and-tested gadget is the microdot which is used to reduce whole pages of information down to a tiny dot. First the document which is to be sent is photographed and the plate exposed on to film. The film is reduced in size so that the final negative is about the size of a colon (:). The agent then writes an innocuous letter using the prepared microdot as part of the standard punctuation. The recipient of the letter can then reverse the process using a microscope and read the message.

Another method for the taking and delivery of messages is the 'dead letter drop.' This involves the use of a pre-arranged

ABOVE: This 'matchbox secret camera' was designed for the use of the OSS in World War II. About 1000 were manufactured by Eastman Kodak, producing a negative a half a square inch in size.

LEFT: Yardley talcum powder cans used by the members of the Portland Spy Ring to hide microfilm and other secret objects. Espionage always depends heavily on miniaturization.

point where two contacts will look if they are instructed that any information is en route. The famous MI6 agent Colonel Oleg Penkovsky used a radiator in a Moscow building as his drop. Frank Bossard, a Soviet agent of the 1950s who was active in the British Ministry of Aviation, used a ruined wall and on other occasions a tree. Another spy, Jean Paul Soupert, a Swiss-born chemical engineer recruited by the East Germans to act in Belgium, used mobile dead letter boxes. Soupert managed to conceal microfilm in toothpaste tubes, bath sponges and even chocolate boxes. The notorious British Portland Spy Ring used

cans of Yardley talcum powder, complete with false bottoms, as part of their communications network.

Electronics plays a major part in the intelligence game, and some of the tricks devised to conceal a 'bug' are highly ingenious. In May 1960 Henry Cabot Lodge, US ambassador to the UN, presented to the National Security Council a wooden carving of the Great Seal of the United States which had been presented to the US embassy in Moscow by Russian guests. The generous gift turned out to be a concealment case for an electronic listening device.

New intakes to the CIA are trained at

Camp Peary in Virginia, nicknamed 'the farm.' While at the farm trainees undergo a rigorous set of tests designed to evaluate the caliber of the agent and also to assess his mental and physical capabilities. Firstly they are taught a form of unarmed combat derived from ju-jitsu, karate, aikido and other martial arts. As part of this physical training the agents are instructed as to where the vulnerable positions on the body are and how to act efficiently and quietly.

The agents also learn about bugging, bag

Bugging has become almost an art, pursued with great subtlety. The handcarved Great Seal of the United States (right), presented to the US ambassador in Moscow by the Soviet Union, turned out to contain a listening device. Telephone bugging (below) was commonplace until phone tapping virtually took its place. A host of devices have been found planted in Western embassies behind the Iron Curtain (below right, a microphone discovered in the Danish embassy in Warsaw; bottom right, a whole collection of electronic gadgets found in the US embassy in Moscow, 1964).

jobs (breaking and entering) and encryption. The area of bugging has now become extremely sophisticated with the use of powerful supercomputers, though there are still occasions when the concealed tape-recorder can prove invaluable. Most security services use a common bug known as an 'infinity bug.' This can be placed anywhere in a suspect's home, pick up all types of activity, and then directly relay this information to a nearby listening post. The bugs are minute, about the size of an olive in a cocktail glass, and are highly efficient. But they are mainly used in low-key intelligence operations. These bugs also used to be placed within telephones to eavesdrop on telephone conversations, but it is now thought that telephone tapping has become so sophisticated that little physical presence is needed. In Britain and the United States telephone tapping is carried out at exchange level, where the engineer simply re-routes the lines which have been ordered to be tapped. The Kray computers can translate the digital message from the telephones and relay the message in analogue (recognizable transcript rather than computer gobbledegook) to the customer or security service which requires the information. The intelligence agencies also spy

on their allies, though they all strongly deny this. In 1975 a Congressional report, the Fink report, detailed that: 'the NSA monitors the traffic of specific countries, including Great Britain our closest ally.' The monitoring of government traffic has been confirmed by a former employee of Vint Hill Farms Station (Warrington, Virginia); the station had a bank of machines and a team of men whose only job was to read and process intercepted British signals.

These communications could have consisted of anything from commercial intelligence to British military communications. The project which set up the Vint Hills operation was curiously known as 'Project Wideband Extraction'; to add insult to injury, the British-based facility at Menwith

Hill, which is staffed by NSA employees, is also connected to Project Wideband. Vint Hills has now been closed down and all operations have been moved to San Antonio, Texas.

Microwave towers, similar to those strange protrusions on London's Post Office Tower, can also be used to intercept communications traffic. The Soviet mission in San Francisco possesses a fine array of aerials on its roof, most of which can be used for eavesdropping. London's Mayfair is also another place where the widespread proliferation of aerials is quite extraordinary; Mayfair is also known as Diplomat-land due to the number of embassies in that area. In 1987 the Senate Intelligence Committee recommended that Soviet diplomats should be forced to quit their new residence on the highest hill in Washington, because it was being used to eavesdrop on US government offices. If all of these facilities are not enough, then look to the sky. The U2 plane was in the iron ages compared to the type of gadgetry now sent up by both the Soviets and the United States. Both countries have excelled with their communications satellites, some of which are powerful enough to send detailed photographs from outer space as well as being able to pick up communications. One danger with all of this sophistication is that governments will use these facilities as much to spy on their own population as to monitor the activities of 'the enemy.' Submarines and ships are also used to pick up

information; sometimes these activities come to light, as when in January 1968 the US spy ship *Pueblo* was captured by North Korean patrol boats off the coast of North Korea.

Whether the vast expenditure on international monitoring is justifiable is another question. Many of the Allied operations duplicate each other or these operations are used as an excuse by both sides to become enmeshed in destabilizing Third World countries, an activity which rapidly becomes costly and bloody.

ABOVE: London's Post Office Tower, topped by microwave receivers of the kind widely used for eavesdropping on communications at home and abroad. The sophistication of much modern long-range listening equipment has made older spy techniques redundant.

CHAPTER 11

CURRENT CONFLICTS

The 1980s have brought no let up in the spy wars between East and West. President Ronald Reagan, who took office in 1981, introduced a new tough US foreign policy that overturned the efforts toward détente and liberalism of the previous decade. The Soviet 'menace' was to be sternly confronted and communism resisted wherever it raised its head. There was a consequent resurgence of covert operations and counter-espionage, once more established as important elements of US policy. For the Soviet Union, technological secrets became the prime target of espionage, as the West's lead in such areas as computers and electronics grew, and Reagan banned the transfer of new technology to the East. Revelations about undercover activities by the CIA, the KGB and other of the world's secret services remained a startlingly prominent feature of the news. The spy business is still big business.

One of Reagan's first acts on becoming president in January 1981 was to begin the rebuilding of the CIA. One of his election campaign promises had been 'to provide our government with the capability to help influence international events vital to our national security interests, a capability which the United States alone among major powers has denied itself.' Covert action was back on the agenda. Reagan appointed a new director of the CIA, William Casey, to replace Stansfield Turner. Casey, a millionaire and a former OSS man, had run the new president's election campaign. His close links with Reagan promised the Agency support from the top. Casey saw his first tasks as building up the strength of the CIA and also increasing its budget. One Congressional intelligence committee member said of Casey: 'He would mount a covert operation in the Vatican if he could.' Such was the new director's zeal for the job.

There were plenty of areas for a revived CIA to work in, notably the supply of arms to

the Mujahidin in Afghanistan and the pursuit of US interests in the war-torn Middle East. But it was in Central America that Casey found both 'the stimulus and the rationale for the resurgence of the CIA.' The flashpoints were Nicaragua, where the left-wing Sandinista regime had come to power in July 1979, overthrowing the dictatorship of Anastasio Somoza Debayle, and neigh-boring El Salvador, in which a guerrilla movement threatened another US-backed government. The US support for the Salvadorean government's counter-insurgency campaign, in which the CIA was certainly involved, proved relatively uncon-troversial, but the determined attempt to subvert the government of Nicaragua was destined eventually to lead to yet another public scandal.

The Sandinista National Liberation Front had been fortunate in that its takeover of power coincided with the Carter Administration in the United States. Carter's

Nicaragua became the first Latin American state to experience a successful guerrilla insurgency since Castro's victory in Cuba when the dictatorship of Anastasio Somoza Debayle (left) was overthrown by the Sandinista National Liberation Front, headed by Daniel Ortega (above), in July 1979.

173

...uary 1980 unarmed demonstrators were
...d on the steps of the cathedral in the capital
...ador; two months later, the popular
...op Oscar Romero was killed by a right-wing
...uad while he was celebrating mass. These
...ts precipitated civil war between an alliance
...d center opposition groups on one side and
...nent forces and right-wingers on the other.
...quickly became involved, assisting
...ent counter-insurgency efforts against what
...picted as a communist attack on a free world
... The new Sandinista government in
...oring Nicaragua was accused of aiding the
...n El Salvador, and this was turned into a public
...tion for President Reagan's backing of the
...guan Contras. The Salvadorean air base at
...o became the center for CIA air operations
...caragua in support of the Contras. The fates of
...ador and Nicaragua seemed inextricably linked
...truggle for Central America.

Images of a deeply divided nation. FAR LEFT: A young masked supporter of the Salvadorean Communist Party. ABOVE LEFT AND CENTER LEFT: The American trained and equipped El Salvador Army. LEFT: An army column ready for action. ABOVE: A guerrilla stands guard in front of a post of the ERP, the Popular Revolutionary Army. TOP: Grieving for victims of a war that shows no signs of ending.

reluctance to support dictators like Somoza left them vulnerable to popular revolt. The new regime at first represented a broad left front ranging from Marxists to liberals, with priests, labor unionists and intellectuals all taking part. But as the government led by Daniel Ortega began to instigate its left-wing policies and rebuilt the country after the ravages of civil war – with the aid of 5000 Cuban technicians, doctors and military personnel – some factions within the country that had supported the overthrow of Somoza became disaffected. In particular, the Catholic church hierarchy adopted a hostile stand, demanding that priests withdraw from participation in the Sandinista regime.

As Ortega's government emerged more clearly in its Marxist colors, President Carter authorized $1 million in secret funding for the middle-of-the-road opposition to the Sandinistas inside Nicaragua. But the Reaganite Republican Party condemned this as overlenient and pledged to better Carter in order to 'support the efforts of the Nicaraguan people to establish a free and independent government.' Less formally, they regarded Nicaragua as a 'second Cuba,' and were determined that this one would not last as long as the first. Soon after his election, Reagan authorized covert military operations in Central America in order to topple the Ortega regime. By November 1981, using as arguments the mounting 'oppression' in Nicaragua (still mild by Latin American standards) and alleged Sandinista support for guerrillas in El Salvador, Reagan persuaded Congress to

ABOVE: Ex-dictator Somoza in exile after his defeat. He lasted little over a year before being assassinated by a bazooka attack in Paraguay in September 1980.

RIGHT: A Contra soldier in training on the Nicaraguan border. President Ronald Reagan was totally dedicated in his support for the Contras in their efforts to invade Nicaragua and overthrow the Sandinista regime.

approve $19.5 million for the CIA to create a commando force to lead a broad anti-Sandinista front. The CIA was also instructed to conduct covert operations against 'Cuban supply lines within Nicaragua.'

The material for the formation of what were to become known as the 'Contras' lay in members of Somoza's National Guard who had taken refuge in Honduras and in the southern United States after the dictator's defeat. The National Guard had been the basis of the Somoza dictatorship and was much hated in Nicaragua, even by those who opposed the Sandinistas' Marxist policies. It was an unlikely instrument for the establishment of a 'free and independent government.' Other exiled opponents of the Sandinistas were pressured by the United States into co-operating with the ex-National Guardsmen, but this fundamental split in the anti-Sandinista movement was never closed.

From early 1981, the CIA set up military training camps in Florida and California to create the anti-Sandinista military force. By

LEFT: A young guerrilla of the ERP revolutionary army in El Salvador, keeping guard with his M16 automatic rifle captured from government forces. The United States accused Nicaragua of aiding the guerrillas in El Salvador and spreading subversion throughout the region.

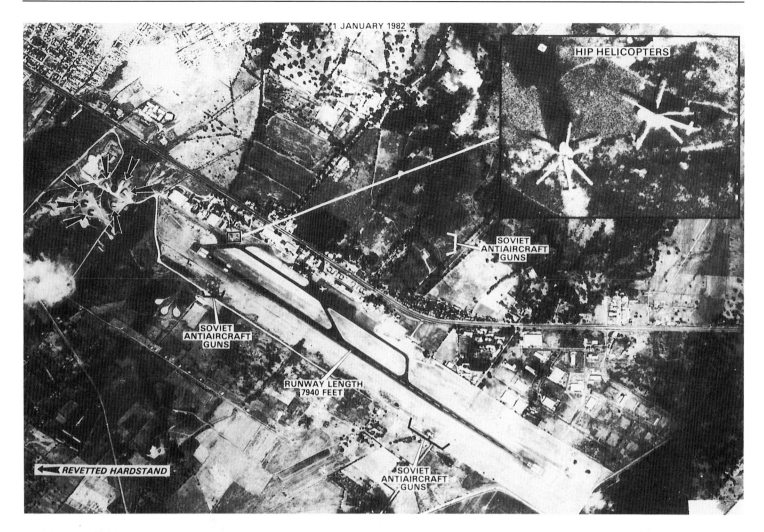

1 JANUARY 1982

HIP HELICOPTERS

SOVIET ANTIAIRCRAFT GUNS

SOVIET ANTIAIRCRAFT GUNS

RUNWAY LENGTH 7940 FEET

◄ REVETTED HARDSTAND

SOVIET ANTIAIRCRAFT GUNS

ABOVE: The CIA mounted repeated spy flights over Nicaragua to monitor military developments and pass on vital information to the Contras. This photo shows developments at Sandino airfield, with the runway being lengthened and anti-aircraft defenses installed. The United States insisted that this was a prelude to the introduction of high-performance Soviet aircraft into Nicaragua, and warned that such a move would be unacceptable. In fact, no Soviet fighters materialized.

the middle of the year General Vernon Walters, former deputy director of the Agency, had arranged the unification of fragmented bands of ex-National Guardsmen for the purpose of raiding Nicaragua from vantage points in Honduras. Funding was also arranged for the Miami-based Nicaraguan Democratic Union (UDN) led by Franciso Cardenal, and the UDN was bribed into joining forces with the newly established military front. This new organization was named the Nicaraguan Democratic Force (FDN). But the CIA failed to persuade Eden Pastora Gomez, a disaffected ex-Sandinista, to link his Costa Rica-based Democratic Revolutionary Alliance (ARDE) to the FDN. To a man such as Pastora, the National Guardsmen were totally unacceptable allies.

In 1982, the Contra war against the Sandinistas hotted up. With funding mounting to some $60 million between 1982 and 1983, the FDN was turned into an army at least 10,000 strong. About 150 CIA operatives were reckoned to be active in their support, and they were involved in much more than training. CIA men organized commando raids on Nicaraguan ports from US vessels, bombing attacks and logistic backing for Contras inside Nicaragua using

aircraft flown by American pilots, and the mining of Nicaraguan coastal waters in an attempted blockade. The revelation of the mining operation, which led to a successful action by the Nicaraguan government against the United States in the World Court at The Hague, was one of a number of disturbing reports that eventually brought about a clampdown on CIA activities. Other factors included evidence of the direct involvement of Americans in military operations inside Nicaragua, and tales of the corruption, inefficiency and criminal activities of Contra leaders. In June 1984 Congress blocked President Reagan's request for extra funding for the Contras, effectively stopping further CIA military support.

Hostility to the CIA operation was reinforced the following October when a CIA manual for subversion was leaked to the press by a Contra leader, Edgar Chamorro, who was opposed to the more extreme ex-National Guard officers of the FDN. Chamorro revealed the existence of an 89-page booklet entitled *Psychological Operations in Guerrilla Warfare*. The booklet advocated assassination, kidnapping, blackmail, mob violence and murder. Chamorro revealed that the booklet had been written for the Contras by the CIA; this

LEFT: Eden Pastora, leader of the Costa-Rica-based ARDE Contra group. A former Sandinista hero who had fallen out with Daniel Ortega, Pastora resisted all American efforts to force him into an alliance with the ex-Somozan National Guard officers of the Honduran-based FDN.

BELOW: The Contras were armed, trained and financed by the CIA, but they proved on the whole disappointing in their military performance. Many stories circulated about the corruption and cruelty of which they were guilty, and allegedly more time was spent in lucrative drug-trafficking operations than in actual fighting.

ABOVE: Lieutenant Colonel Oliver North takes the oath before the Foreign Affairs Committee examining the Irangate scandal. North was prominent in dealings both with the Contras and the Iran government.

was initially denied by the Reagan Administration, but *Newsweek* learned that top White House planners were involved in the production of the manual, including UN delegate Jeanne Kirkpatrick. Sections of the pamphlet which so incensed Congress include paragraphs recommending the use of 'professional criminals' to 'be hired to take the demonstrators to a confrontation with the authorities to bring about uprisings and shootings that will create a martyr. It is

possible to neutralize carefully selected and planned targets such as court judges and security officials but it is absolutely necessary to gather together the population affected so that they will take part.' After these revelations Chamorro was dumped by the Agency, but the damage was done. In 1985 Congress totally suspended overt aid, military or humanitarian, to the Contras.

After the traumas of the 1970s, the CIA was reluctant to continue its operations against the Sandinista regime illegally, but the Reagan Administration was still determined that the Contras should be supported. The National Security Council stepped into the breach, through co-ordinator Lieutenant Colonel Oliver North. North visited rebel camps in his own aircraft and personally assured the Contras that 'Reagan would publicly endorse Contra efforts to remove the Sandinistas from power and see to it that the Contras had all the support necessary.' Funds were collected through a network of extreme rightwing groups in the United States, including the Soldiers of Fortune, the Friends of America, the Dooley Foundation and the World Anti-Communist League. A network of ex-CIA officers became involved in the operation, including pilots who had flown with Air America in Laos, now back on missions over Nicaragua, flying out of the Salvadorean air base of Ilopango. A retired

LEFT: US troops keep guard over Grenadian and Cuban prisoners after the American invasion of Grenada in October 1983. The aggressive foreign policy of the Reagan Administration was immensely popular in the United States, even if it sometimes distressed America's allies.

When it was first revealed that the National Security Council had organized clandestine arms shipments to Iran and made arrangements for continuing military supplies to the Contras despite a Congressional ban, President Reagan (right) denied all knowledge of the operation, while his National Security Advisor Vice Admiral John Poindexter (below) was one of those to take the rap.

air force general, Richard Secord, who had also taken part in the Laos operation and was now head of the Stanford Technology Trading Group, provided much of the organization for North's covert effort to keep the Contras supplied, financed and otherwise supported. By mid-1986, Secord and North estimated that the value of their 'assets' in the Contra supply operation was around $4.5 million.

By the time Congress agreed to restore official funding to the Contras in August 1986, North's Nicaraguan venture was entangled in an apparently separate covert operation, a secret arms deal with Iran. By the end of 1986 this had become public, creating the 'Irangate' scandal, that threatened to rock US political life in the same way Watergate had in the previous decade. As revelation followed revelation, a provisional picture of the murky Iran deal could be made out even before the major public investigation opened in May 1987.

ABOVE: Americans in Lebanon were very exposed to attacks by Islamic extremists, and the CIA proved no exception. The Stars and Stripes here fly over the rubble of the US embassy in Beirut, hit by a suicide bomb attack in April 1983 that killed 60 people, including at least seven CIA operatives.

leased and, despite President Reagan's public stance that there would be no deal with terrorists, moves began to organize a swap of hostages for arms – vitally needed by Iran for its war against Iraq. There was an official US embargo on arms sales to Iran, but military equipment had been filtering through by a number of routes, especially with the connivance of Israel, for its own contorted diplomatic motives. The Israelis were willing to provide the first of the 'arms-for-hostages' deliveries to Iran in late 1985 as the negotiations got under way. But by early 1986 the National Security Council had organized its own supply network, involving Oliver North, Richard Secord, an airline formerly owned by the CIA, Southern Air Transport, and various international arms dealers. By this time Buckley was dead, succumbing to the strain of captivity and torture, but there were still other hostages to rescue, and there was the question of 'buying back' secrets, such as the identity of CIA agents in the Middle East, that Buckley apparently had revealed during his brutal interrogation.

The first direct US arms shipment went to Iran in February 1986, followed by a second in May, when both North and national security advisor Robert McFarlane went along for talks with Iranian leaders. The final shipment was made on 29 October 1986, after which US hostage David Jacobsen was finally released. It was not much of a reward for so much effort. However, there had allegedly been a spin-off from the Iran arms deal: the profits from the transaction were apparently used to finance military supplies for the Contras in Honduras.

Although much remained obscure, revelations about the illegal supply of arms to Iran and to the Contras threw the Reagan Administration and the intelligence community into turmoil in late 1986. For William Casey, it was too much to bear: he was struck down by a brain tumor in December and died the following year. Deputy director Robert Gates was originally chosen to succeed to the directorship, but despite the CIA's efforts to distance itself from the illegal arms operations, Gates was considered too involved in the scandal to be confirmed in the post. William H Webster, the FBI chief, was eventually shifted across to head the CIA. Meanwhile the Contra war continued to cause massive suffering in Nicaragua, but without showing any signs of weakening the Sandinista regime. If anything, the acts of aggression carried out by the Contras against civilian as well as military targets caused opposing factions to unite in the country's defense.

The overthrow of the US-backed Shah of Iran by the followers of the Ayatollah Khomeni in 1979 had seriously weakened America's position in the Middle East and the aggressive anti-Americanism of pro-Iranian Islamic groups in other countries in the region led to further setbacks, especially for the CIA. In April 1983 the US embassy in Beirut, Lebanon, was badly damaged in a suicide bomb attack by an Islamic extremist. Among the 60 people killed were at least seven CIA men, including the station chief Robert Ames. Even worse followed. In March 1984, Ames' replacement, William Buckley, was kidnapped outside his Beirut appartment and held along with other hostages by an Iranian-backed group. The US Administration and the CIA were frantic to get Buckley and the other hostages re-

The KGB, naturally, went through no such public traumas. During Andropov's short reign as Soviet leader, Viktor Chebrikov became chairman of the KGB, and he was confirmed in the position by Mikhail Gorbachev. In April 1985, Chebrikov was made a full member of the ruling politburo. Some commentators saw a clash of interests between the security service and Gorbachev's liberalizing policy of *glasnost*. But in so far as Gorbachev intended to attack corruption in the Communist Party and amongst the managerial class, he could probably expect the whole-hearted support of the KGB, already identified with campaigns to clean up Soviet society. As always, however, the inner workings of the Soviet system remained carefully hidden.

LEFT: Mikhail Gorbachev, the Soviet leader whose dynamic approach to the problems of bureaucracy and economic inefficiency offered hope of change in the fossilized communist state.

LEFT: An advertisement for job applicants to take up a career in the CIA. Ten years earlier very few graduates would have thought of joining the discredited Agency, but by 1986 it had once more achieved public respectability as necessary to the defense of US interests. Nevertheless, CIA recruitment campaigns on American campuses did provoke some reaction by student protesters who had not forgotten the experiences and attitudes of the 1960s and 1970s.

The late 1970s and early 1980s saw a concerted drive by the KGB to gain the latest Western technological secrets. The Soviets had the capacity to develop computers but were unable to produce their own microchip. They were heavily dependent on anything the West would export, and when the West decided that certain developments were too militarily sensitive to export to the Soviet Union, the Soviets had to depend on illegal methods of obtaining the technology they needed.

In 1981 the FBI estimated that 35 percent of official Soviet representatives working within the United States were officers of the KGB or the GRU (military intelligence). Principal areas of activity include Washington, New York and San Francisco, where each Soviet installation has been chosen to maximize electronic surveillance. The Washington-based Soviet embassy used to boast one huge high-frequency antenna on its roof, part of which pointed toward the Pentagon and the White House, the other toward Langley Virginia. The Soviets have deliberately chosen Chesapeake Bay as their recreational base since it is right next door to the Annapolis military microwave relay station. The Riverdale, New York, residential complex has on its roof a complex array of electronic gadgetry specifically

designed to pick up US communications traffic, while the Soviets' San Francisco consulate can pick up information from both 'Silicon Valley' and Mare Island, a US nuclear submarine base. The men chosen for the KGB's US activities are, in the words of FBI officer Theodore Gardiner, 'the cream of the crop.' The one-time head of the KGB in Washington, Dmitry Yakushkin, has been identified as the grandson of a general of the December 1917 revolution. The New York KGB chief, Vladimir Kazkov, is an ex-head of the First Department, Moscow. The Soviet embassy in Washington provides a useful idea of how the KGB operates within the United States. A general operations section provides vital contact with the GRU and is actively involved in recruiting possible US agents. A lot of time is spent hanging around in bars which proliferate near military bases. Up-market clubs are joined in an effort to gain access to highly classified information; also libraries are combed for important but unclassified information which exists in the fields of science and technology. Money is the main impetus in recruitment rather than the ideals that motivated an earlier generation. Former CIA officer Harry Rositzke claims: 'The average American soberly regards money as the sole means of ensuring personal freedom and independence ... This attitude towards money engenders an indifference to the means by which it is obtained.' One agent who was tempted by the financial rewards of working for the KGB was William Holden Bell, a Hughes aircraft engineer. The Polish agent Zacharsky also persuaded Bell that violent acts would be carried out against his family unless he complied with requests for information. It was through Bell that the FBI learnt about Soviet interest in Silicon Valley.

Silicon Valley is an area near San Francisco where over 600 companies work on classified government hi-tech projects. A similar facility exists near Los Angeles with a further 350 companies. The KGB has a conveniently placed West Coast headquarters in its San Francisco consulate staffed, according to FBI estimates, by about 60 KGB officers and a further 25 members of the GRU. Some officials are actively involved in the procurement of sensitive hi-tech secrets, but frequently their work is done for them by greedy Western businessmen.

In 1981 a Soviet-born US citizen, Anatoly Maluta, was convicted on charges of illegally exporting $8-10 million of computers and electronic equipment to the Soviet Union. Actively involved in the fight against hi-tech spies were the Departments of

RIGHT: The Soviet embassy in Washington, a center for intelligence activities aimed at American technological, political and military secrets. The hi-frequency antenna on the roof was reputedly used to listen in to government communications.

Commerce and Customs. It was an agent from Commerce who first became suspicious about Maluta's activities, mainly through the activities of another alleged smuggler, Werner Bruchhausen, a West German millionaire. Bruchhausen had been implicated in various cases involving the violation of US export controls; it was alleged that Bruchhausen had been actively involved in re-exporting US technology to the Soviet bloc. Bruchhausen's chief US associate was Anatoly Maluta. The Commerce officials checked up on Maluta and discovered that among the orders that Maluta had on his books was a request for four microwave and antenna systems. Initially Maluta claimed that the US Army's Communications Command and Army Intelligence school at Fort Huachuca had placed these orders, but the claim was strongly denied by the Army. Commerce later discovered that the orders were destined for the Soviet Union through a complex array of cover companies and intricate European smuggling routes. Maluta was sentenced to five years imprisonment for his activities.

In the early 1980s over 90 Soviet agents were expelled from their base countries for varying degrees of intelligence-gathering.

Forty-seven were expelled from France, four from Britain, four from Italy, 18 from Iran and three from the United States. The Belgians expelled Yevgeny Mikhailov, director-general of a Belgian/Soviet trade company, in 1983. Further expulsions, especially by the United States, continued into the second half of the 1980s, provoking tit-for-tat expulsion of Western diplomats from Moscow.

In 1986 the United States was stunned to discover that a former CIA agent, Edward Lee Howard, had defected to Moscow. US newspapers claimed that a US contact in Moscow had already been killed because of information leaked by Howard. The CIA and the FBI came under fierce attack in the United States for allowing Howard to slip out of the country. It had been known for at least two years that Howard was a KGB spy, thanks to information received from the Soviet defector Vitaly Yurchenko. Howard had managed to leave his Santa Fe home by simply putting a dummy in his car which lulled the FBI watchers into a false sense of security, thus giving Howard the freedom to escape from his house through a back exit.

Further Soviet spying activities in the United States came to light with the 1986 capture of Gennadi Zakharov. Zakharov was

ABOVE: The US embassy building in Moscow. Among the problems encountered by staff there was at one time the bombardment of the building with ultra frequency radiation as part of a Soviet bugging operation, leading to a serious health risk.

RIGHT: US journalist Nicholas Daniloff, who was arrested as a spy by the KGB in 1986. The main purpose of Daniloff's arrest was almost certainly to obtain the release of Soviet spy Gennadi Zakharov, being held in the United States, in a spy swap. But the sort of 'investigative reporting' conducted by Western journalists often amounts to espionage in a Soviet context – the seeking out of facts that the government does not want publicly known.

ton, on which the United States and the Soviet Union had agreed over a decade earlier. In 1987, the chancery building in the new US embassy in Moscow was declared unusable because it had been so successfully planted with bugging devices during its construction. At the same time, US Congressmen moved to stop the Soviets occupying their new residence in Washington, because it was reportedly a center for electronic espionage on US government buildings.

a Soviet physicist assigned to the United Nations Secretariat, one of about 300 Soviet officials who work at the Secretariat. It was alleged that Zakharov was involved in spying activities and he was actually captured whilst in the process of handing over $1000 to an American employee of a US defense contractor. Zakharov had lived in the United States since 1982 and by all accounts was the model neighbor, kind, courteous and very quiet. It came as something of a shock for his neighbors to discover that FBI officials examining Zakharov's flat had found communications equipment, details of other foreign espionage agents and records of payments made to these agents. As with Maluta, Zakharov's main areas of interest were connected with the US hi-technology machine. Zakharov was 'spy-swapped' for US journalist Nicholas Daniloff, who had been picked up by the KGB purportedly for espionage in the Soviet Union. In fact, the arrest of Daniloff was probably specifically designed to give the Soviets a bargaining counter to get Zakharov back.

The Zakharov-Danilov deal immediately preceded a summit meeting between President Reagan and Gorbachev at Reykjavik, Iceland, and through 1986 and the start of 1987 there was a strong interplay of on the one hand moves toward détente and an arms agreement between the superpowers, and on the other a ruthless pursuit of the espionage and counter-espionage war. A focus for the spy war was the building of new embassies in Moscow and Washing-

Meanwhile, Africa continued to be an active field for intelligence activity. In 1986 it was revealed that the CIA had been propping up the South African apartheid regime by giving the South African government information on the exiled African National Congress (ANC). The ANC has been a proscribed organization within South Africa since 1960, but has continued to operate underground, giving support to the black struggle within South Africa. Its leader, Nelson Mandela, has languished in prison since 1962. The main excuse used by

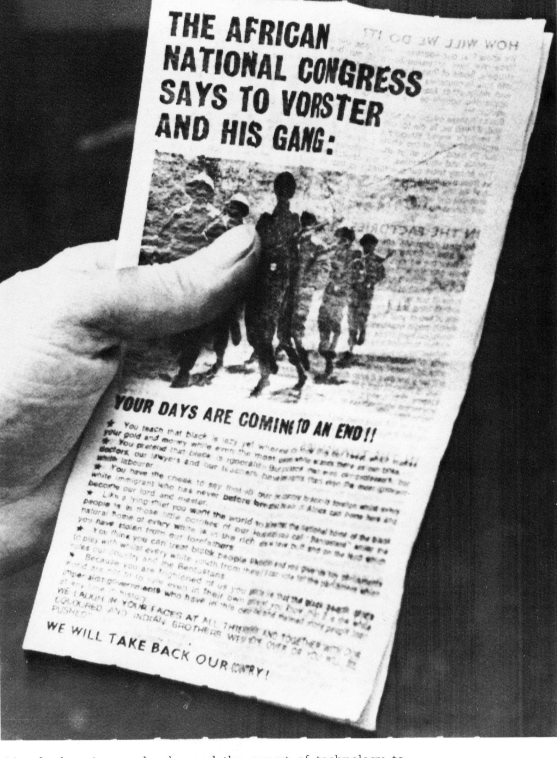

LEFT: Nelson Mandela, the most famous prisoner of the South African regime. He has been jailed since 1962 for his role as leader of the black revolutionary movement, the ANC.

RIGHT: An African National Congress (ANC) leaflet addresses the white regime. The CIA and British secret services have co-operated with the South Africans against the ANC, despite the rather different public stance of the American and British governments.

the South African authorities for banning the ANC was that the organization was communist and made up of terrorists. To be found guilty of belonging to the ANC can lead to long imprisonment and even torture. Right-wingers within the Reagan Administration seized upon the allegations that the ANC was dominated by communists and used this as an excuse to pass on information about the organization to Pretoria. This policy is a complete reversal of the Carter Administration's ban on any information-sharing with Pretoria. Publicly Carter had

also banned the export of technology to South Africa but Administration officials have admitted that quantities of electronic equipment, including antennas and interception receivers, were shipped to South Africa via Britain and West Germany.

In 1984 the British and representatives from the NSA attended a high-level meeting at Britain's GCHQ. At this meeting the two sides reviewed previous intelligence assignments and future targets, and later South African military intelligence officers were ushered into the room. The United

States and Britain requested that South Africa continue to monitor Soviet and Cuban activity in Angola and Mozambique, as well as Soviet submarine activity around the Cape of Good Hope. The South Africans were also asked if they could provide information on Soviet activity south of the Sahara and Soviet support for the South-West African Peoples' Organization (SWAPO) in Namibia, against whom South Africa has been involved in a long and

RIGHT: Oliver Tambo, the exiled president of the ANC. The South African intelligence services were anxious for information on Tambo from the CIA, and were prepared to monitor Soviet military activity in southern Africa as a quid pro quo.

bloody war. In return the South Africans asked the two powers to relay any intercepted information concerning the governments of Mozambique, Angola, Botswana, Zambia and military activity south of the Sahara. The South Africans also wanted information on the movements of ANC deputy, Oliver Tambo, and any South African exiles who aided and supported the ANC. The South Africans asked the United States and Britain to monitor communications between the different groups of the ANC, and GCHQ agreed to monitor these activities in Zambia, where there is a large ANC base.

Some US officials denied that this meeting had ever taken place, but others, including right-wing Senator Jesse Helms, supported such action in view of CIA reports which held that the ANC was dominated by communists. As far as it is possible to judge, such intelligence-sharing activities still continue despite the growing Western horror at the apartheid system.

Another area where the CIA and the

British intelligence forces have joined up is in the troubled province of Northern Ireland. Mainly under the pretext of Nato membership the intelligence forces have combined to provide an extremely sophisticated array of listening devices the length and breadth of both Northern Ireland and the neutral Irish Republic. The CIA also helps the British government out with information about suspected members of the Provisional Irish Republican Army (IRA).

Security operations in Northern Ireland have brought out sharp rivalries between the British secret services. As befits its internal security role, MI5 has mostly handled the province, in collaboration with the Special Branch of the Royal Ulster Constabulary (RUC). But in the mid-1970s, MI6 was also involved in intelligence operations there, and in 1979 ex-MI6 chief Sir Maurice Oldfield was made security co-ordinator for Northern Ireland. As we have already said, rumors of Sir Maurice's homosexual indiscretions were reportedly circulated by MI5 to get him removed from the job. MI5 always preferred a free hand, and it may also have been behind the removal of another intruder on the scene, the Deputy Chief Constable of Manchester, John Stalker. This

senior British police officer was empowered to investigate charges that the security forces were carrying out a 'shoot-to-kill' policy in Northern Ireland, through which unarmed suspects had been gunned down. Stalker was making important progress in his investigation when an intimidating smear campaign of uncertain origin led to his suspension from duties. He was found not guilty of the charges arising out of the smear campaign but was not allowed to continue his enquiries into the RUC. Some newspapers speculated that MI5 was behind the campaign to have Stalker removed from the case.

Far more sensational allegations against MI5 emerged in 1987, however, through the writings of an ex-MI5 officer, Peter Wright. In his book *Spycatcher* he not only repeated the charge that Sir Roger Hollis, the head of MI5 from 1956 to 1965, had been a Soviet spy – a view already expressed in Chapman Pincher's book *Their Trade is Treachery*, but also claimed that 30 of his MI5 colleagues had conspired to destablize the Labour government of Harold Wilson in 1974. These MI5 men apparently believed that Wilson himself was a Soviet agent, and that his predecessor as head of the Labour

LEFT: Senior British police officer John Stalker was given the task of investigating allegations that the security forces in Northern Ireland had killed unarmed men suspected of involvement with the IRA. It is widely believed that MI5 was responsible for a smear campaign which forced Stalker off the case and, eventually, out of the police force.

Party, Hugh Gaitskell, had been assassinated by the KGB in 1963 to allow Wilson to assume the leadership.

The British government of Margaret Thatcher went to extraordinary lengths to prevent the publication of Wright's allegations, and it is perhaps this above all else that lends them a degree of credence. Wright attempted to have the book published in Australia, but after taking out an injunction against the Australian publisher, the British government fought the case through the Australian courts. Sir Robert

LEFT: Relatives and friends protest at the deaths of three Northern Ireland Catholics killed by the security forces. No weapons were found in their car after the shooting (above).

RIGHT: Former MI5 operative Peter Wright whose book *Spycatcher* contained some startling allegations about the British secret service. Prime Minister Margaret Thatcher was determined to stop publication of the book, but no more determined than was Wright to see it published. The Wright affair brought into the open the direct conflict between the secrecy of the intelligence services and the need for open government in a democracy.

Armstrong, a member of the Joint Intelligence Committee, was briefed to defend the government line, and at one point in the case was forced to admit that, if not lying, he may at least have been 'economical with the truth.'

In fact that phrase 'economical with the truth' can be used to describe the clandestine nature of the operations of all intelligence agencies. In some cases they work for the good of the nation and act in a responsible and effective manner. In other cases, however, the agencies seem to become increasingly absorbed with their own importance and fail to recognize that they should be first and foremost directed by the government which they serve and not embark on autonomous mini-wars against countries or individuals which meet with their displeasure. When they carry out activities which are not in line with policies of the government of the day they should be totally answerable for these operations and never be allowed to shield behind the catch-all phrase of 'activities carried out in the interests of national security.'

Index

Acknowledgments

The Publisher would like to thank Adrian Gilbert and Reg Grant who edited the book, Design 23 who designed it, Melanie Earnshaw who carried out the picture research and Ron Watson who compiled the index. We would also like to thank the following picture agencies, institutions and individuals for supplying the illustrations on the pages noted:

Aid to Russian Christians: page 150
Associated Press: pages 12(top left), 20, 27(below), 33, 37, 40(both), 41(top), 42-43(top), 50, 54(top), 56, 72(below), 78(both), 80 84, 85, 86(top), 90(top), 95(top), 103(below), 105(top), 109(below), 111(below), 114, 117(both top), 120(top), 124-125(both) 131(below), 136(both), 143(below), 156, 157(top), 169(below), 170(both), 171(left), 173, 180(below), 181(below), 182, 184, 187, 190
BBC/Bettmann Archive: pages 26(below), 30-31(all 4), 51(below), 58(below), 64(top), 101, 140, 176(below), 179(top)
Bison Picture Library: pages 10(all 3), 11(top), 62(2 below),

63(both), 96, 113(top), 120(below), 121(below), 138(2 below), 166(right), 167(below left & right), 178, 180(top), 183
Camera Press: pages 7(top), 14(below), 16(below), 18, 18-19(top), 28, 29, 32, 34-35, 36, 39(both), 41(below), 42(left), 48(top), 49(both), 51(top), 55, 59, 61(top), 62(top), 65(top), 66(top), 70(right), 71(top), 73(top), 75, 79(both), 87(top), 88, 89, 90(below), 94, 95(below), 98-99, 99(below), 100, 103(top), 104(both), 106, 107, 118-119, 123, 127(below), 128, 129(top), 131(top), 132(below), 134(top), 135, 137(below), 141(top), 143(below), 145(both top), 148(below), 149(both), 151(left), 152, 154-155(all 5), 158(top), 164(both), 165, 174-175(all 6), 176(top), 177, 179(below), 183(top), 186(both), 189(top)
Chile Solidarity Campaign: page 134(below)
Communication Control Systems: page 163(both)
Joe Coughlan: page 171(right)
London Express News Services: page 160, 172(top)
John Frost Newspapers: page 161
Sheila Gray/Format: page 69(both)
Ana Gonzales/Oxfam: page 57(both)
Greek Embassy: page 25(top)
Robert Hunt Picture Library: page 21
Imperial War Museum, London: pages 8(top), 23(both), 25 (below)
Pacemaker Press: pages 153(both), 188-189(below & right)
Photri: pages 43(below), 44, 46(below), 47(below), 65(below), 66(below), 76(centre), 77(below), 98(both), 99(top), 139(all 3), 141(below), 142, 166(top), 181(top)
The Press Association: page 74(top left)
South African Military Information Bureau: page 91(right)
John Massey Stewart: pages 13(below), 48(below), 146-147
TPS/Central Press: pages 12(below right), 83(above), 87(below), 91(left), 112, 168(below)
TPS/Fox Photos: pages 7(below), 14(above), 76(top)
TPS/Keystone: pages 8(below), 9, 11(2 below), 15, 16(top), 17(both), 19(below), 24(below), 26(top), 27(top), 45, 53(both), 54(below), 55, 61(below), 64(below), 67, 70(left), 71(right), 73(below), 74(top right & below), 76(below), 77(top), 81, 83(below), 86(below), 92-93, 97, 102(both) 105(below), 108, 109(top), 110, 111(top), 113(below), 115, 116, 117(below), 126, 127(above), 129(below), 130, 132(top), 133, 137(top), 145(below), 148(top), 151(right), 157(below), 159, 162(below), 168(top), 169(top)
TPS/Three Lions: pages 118(top), 122
TRH: pages 46(top), 47(top), 121(both top), 123(top), 166(left), 167(top)
TRH/Robin Adshead: page 146(below)
US Department of State: page 170(top)
US National Archives: page 158(below)